slices of life

a minnesota memoir

Donna Schilling

X-presso books

Slices of life: a Minnesota memoir

Cover photograph by Thomas D. Jones
Cover & interior design by Tony Dierckins

About the cover:
"Slices of Life" is served with butter freshly turned out of
Grandmother Randi Heieie's mold with carved acorn motif, circa 1870.
It is presented on Aunt Alma Heieie's Bavarian china butter dish, circa 1930.

The photographs in this book are from the author's family album.

First Edition, 2006
06 07 08 09 10 • 5 4 3 2 1

Library of Congress Control Number: 2006930304

Softcover ISBNs: 1-887317-75-9

Printed in Minnesota, U.S.A.

Contact the author at:
2 North 58TH Avenue East
Duluth, Minnesota 55804
218-525-1012

Published through

X-presso
books

Duluth, Minnesota, USA • www.x-communication.org

For My Parents, Alice and William Ferdon

∿

The author would like to thank....

My siblings, Jerry Ferdon, Wanda Jones, and Yvonne Dohr,
for offering their recollections without correcting mine.

My children, Hartley and Dawn Schilling,
for their encouragement and guidance through the
bewildering world of computer technology.

Mara Hart, my first writing teacher,
who has become my close friend and mentor.

My "writing family" of Lake Superior Writers memoir group—
Martha Aas, Kay Coventry, Jeanice Fontaine, Destri Irwin,
Margaret Kinetz, Dorothy Lutz, and Shirley Wuchter—
for seven years of reading and critiquing my stories.

My dear friend Joan Smith, who enrolled me in
and accompanied me to my first writing class.

Thomas D. Jones, the photographer who created
the still life photo gracing the cover of this book, as well as
reproductions of pictures in the photo gallery section inside.

Tony Dierckins of X-Communication for his patience
and dedicated effort in overall layout and cover design,
as well as seeing the book through printing and production.

Claryce Swensen and Dawn Schilling,
who took on the tedious task of proofreading to
help maintain the book's quality and integrity.

Contents

Part 5: Bread Pudding

Part 6: The Ingredients

Preface

began writing this collection of memoirs in 1975 when a niece asked me to write everything I could remember about our family to assist her in a school project. I wrote profiles of each member of Mother's family and each member of Dad's family to the best of my recollection. Soon, family members were asking for copies of these profiles, and as time went on I acquired additional information to add to the sketches. The profiles appear as Part Six of this book.

When I discovered how little we knew about some of our family members and realized there was no one left to ask, I was prompted to begin recording some details of the lives of people in my own generation. After attending writing classes, joining Lake Superior Writers, and working with a group of memoir writers, I found I was completely absorbed in the stories of people and places I had known in my lifetime in addition to our family stories.

I was not so much interested in genealogy as I was creating small vignettes from our life stories to share with our family (especially the younger generations) some of our joy and pain as we lived in the rapidly changing twentieth and twenty first centuries.

The memoirs were randomly created as I recalled them, and Parts One through Five separate them by various periods in my life. In some cases, I enlisted the help of my siblings to recreate events I was too young to recall.

Perhaps in later years, this collection will inspire family members of future generations to add their own memoirs of people and places they knew and loved.

— *Donna Schilling*

Part One:

Mixing the Dough

Child of the Thirties

Grandma Ferdon never let me forget that she brought me into this world and saved my life by removing the umbilical cord which had become wrapped around my neck. Grandma was a hard-bitten woman who had been transplanted at an early age from upstate New York to Minnesota.

On September 17, 1933, the day of my birth, Grandma had been at our house for a few days anticipating the arrival of the third child of her son William and his wife Alice, when they were thirty two and thirty four years of age respectively. Their family to that date consisted of a seven year old son, Gerald, and his sister, Wanda, four years his junior.

It was early morning, ahead of the predicted date, when the doctor was called to our rural home which my family had named *The Meadow Place*, near Osakis, Minnesota to attend my birth. As Grandma often described the scene to me through my early years, she took charge realizing that the doctor was not going to be there for my arrival.

"You were just so impatient to get into this world, you couldn't wait for the doctor," Grandma told me.

She was no stranger to home birthing, and in the country settings where she had lived most of her life, doctors often arrived later than the babies they were to deliver. I weighed in at six and one-half pounds, according to the hand-held spring scale Daddy used to weigh fish. I was placed in a diaper with the corners knotted securely to fit over the hook at the bottom of the scale.

I know I was not beautiful because I remember Mother's rapturous descriptions of how perfect my sister had been as a baby. Her only comment about my appearance was that I was scrawny.

Somehow I concluded at an early age that it was unlikely anyone was thrilled at the prospect of a third child in the midst of the depression following the stock market crash of 1929. I know that Mother worked hard and didn't have much time to spend with me. I recall trying to do things to help hoping to receive acknowledgement that I was of some value to the family. When no affirmation was forthcoming, I commented, "I guess you're pretty lucky to have me, aren't you?"

But since the only response was laughter, I concluded they didn't feel particularly lucky.

We moved shortly after my birth, so I don't remember The Meadow Place. Mother must have hated it because she said to me years later, "I worked so hard before you were born trying to keep that house clean. The floors were rough and nearly impossible to keep up. I'm sure that's why you always want everything just so."

She was convinced that a mother's stress and anxiety exerted an influence on her unborn children which were later manifested on their personalities.

Our next home was the house on the "hill road" in another sparsely populated rural area near Long Prairie, Minnesota. The living room was furnished with a nickel-trimmed wood-burning stove, horsehair upholstered sofa and wooden rocking chair with a worn brown leather seat. A library table and a couple of straight-backed oak chairs, along with a fern on a tall plant stand filled the remainder of the space. Lace curtains at the windows and Mother's hand-crocheted doilies provided the only touches of softness to the room. The curtains were backed by dark green roller shades.

Our kitchen was dominated by a great iron cookstove which featured a shelf across the top with doors that rolled down to keep food warm until serving time. There was a reservoir on the side to heat water and a griddle in the center, flanked by four other large lids upon which to place cooking pots. The stovetop was heated by burning wood beneath the lids, which were removed with a lifter to add the required number of sticks to attain the proper temperature. Mother could determine exactly how many sticks to add by placing her hand above the lid for a few seconds. The oven was heated by wood-burning chambers beneath it. On the adjacent wall a large wooden cabinet was topped by a cupboard containing glassware and china.

A bin for flour, a side door for pots and pans, and drawers for flatware and other utensils comprised the lower cabinet.

A washstand on the wall opposite the stove served various purposes; it held dishpans at dishwashing time, a washbasin for morning and evening hand and face washings, and a covered container of drinking and cooking water. On Mondays, the washstand took center stage when washtubs and wringer came out of the shed off the back door to take their place at weekly laundry time. Breakfast and lunch were served on a wooden oilcloth-covered kitchen table. A pantry off the kitchen held large utensils for cooking and canning, along with other canning supplies. The lower shelves contained gleaming rows of jewel colored canned goods preserved in Mason jars. The fruits and vegetables harvested during the previous summer were carefully preserved to carry us through the long winter.

The family congregated at the round oak table in the dining room for our evening meal. A matching buffet was topped by one of Mother's embroidered scarves and held table linens and serving dishes. After we had finished dinner and washed the dishes, we returned to the dining room table to do our schoolwork by lamplight.

The downstairs bedroom where our parents slept was furnished with a painted iron bed and wooden dresser painted to match. A small bedstand held a kerosene lamp and windup alarm clock. One of the upstairs bedrooms was occupied by my brother, and the other by my older sister and me. A few years later, a younger sister joined us.

A small stuffy attic which could be reached from the upstairs hall was important to us as it held Mother's trunk and picture box. The trunk held her youthful treasures from less stressful days in the carefree "Roaring Twenties" and, along with the large box of family photos, revealed its contents to amuse us on long winter days. Only Mother was allowed access to this space, and its treasures were made available to us at her discretion, so we were amazed at each new presentation and its story. The box of studio photos also contained Mother's album of snapshots taken with her Eastman Brownie camera, now disabled, but still reposing in her trunk in the hope of repair at some future date.

The depression had taken its toll to one degree or another on everyone we knew. We didn't see people living lavishly so didn't feel deprived. We were able to discern, by poring over the Sears catalogue, that some people must have money to buy the wonderful merchandise displayed on its pages, but they weren't people we knew.

We felt secure in our family circle. I couldn't imagine what it would be like to not have both parents. It would never have occurred to me to worry about my parents separating, as I simply did not know anything about divorce. When Mother and Daddy openly disagreed about something, it didn't feel good, but it was not a source of real concern. My older sister recalls tension between our parents at that time, possibly as a result of Mother's complaints about "being stuck out here in the sticks." She had spent most of her life on a farm near Greenbush, Minnesota, escaping only when she grew up and found a job as a telephone operator in St. Paul. She was living there at the Y.W.C.A. when she met and married my father. Now it appeared she was back in the same boat.

Mother's sister, Alma, who lived in Minneapolis, managed a home at White Bear Lake for a member of the wealthy James Hill railroad family. The family had girls just our ages, whose outgrown, barely worn clothing often came our way, as Aunt Alma was responsible for supervising the disposition of outgrown or unused items. We quickly developed a preference for fine batiste nightgowns and simply, but beautifully designed dresses and coats. Unused lengths of fabric were often relegated to the boxes of clothing earmarked for disposal. Mother, an excellent seamstress, turned these windfalls into clothing for us. She fashioned patterns from tissue paper to use in creating her own designs.

She was also a great storyteller, a blessing since we had few books and lived miles from the nearest library. We liked Mother's stories better anyway. She sometimes told them in Norwegian, which we didn't understand, but shouted with laughter at the funny sounding language. Our favorite story in Norwegian was *Billy Goats Gruff*, which would be retold many years later (in response to our pleas) for our children, to their delight. Perhaps Mother welcomed this brief return to her family's native tongue. Her family had spoken Norwegian at home, and she learned English from her older siblings and at school.

I walked at ten months and, according to Mother, she had a hard time correcting my determination that my daily 6 A.M. chore was to empty the kitchen cabinet where the cookware was stored. Early in life, I decided that I was a disappointment to Mother, but there was no question about Daddy's approval. I ran to meet him every evening on his return from his job on a road crew, running as fast as I could down the long driveway so I could jump on the running board of the car to ride back to the house with the soft leaves from the shrubs along the drive brushing me as I clung to the side of the car. Quick-moving, and quick-thinking, I was Daddy's girl and he nick-named me "Speed."

One of my earliest memories is of Daddy teasing me, trying to make me laugh to forget something I was fussing about. Evidently I was old enough to talk because I remember saying, "I'll pop you in the eye if you don't stop that!"

He didn't, and I did. My fist just fit in his eye which became red and watery before it turned black and blue. He simply said, "You warned me," and then laughed long and loudly. I, on the other hand, felt awful as I viewed the watering, injured eye. Mother didn't laugh and appeared ready to mete out punishment, but Daddy said, "No, I asked for it." I think he was secretly proud of me.

Many of the stories I have included in this collection tell about my early years in this setting with my parents and three siblings.

Always aware of the connection between Grandma and myself, I wondered if that umbilical cord she removed from my neck bound us together forever. If so, could it be possible that when she died, I'd go with her? This uneasy childhood flight of fancy disappeared long before Grandma died over thirty years ago at ninety four years of age.

∾

Haying Season

*T*he following image was an unexpected gift, its value limited only by the boundaries of my imagination. It was presented to me in a conversation with my brother when he was well over seventy and my sixties were waning. I had asked him to tell me what his life had been like before I was born. This is my perception of the earliest memory that came to his mind:

~

The year is 1929. Picture, if you will, a three year old boy running through an endless field of hay. He creates a mere ripple of a swath in the lush crop. His tousled hair becomes one with the hay as the sun transforms all to shimmering gold. The hay moves in gentle response to a slight breeze. The child is propelled by pent-up energy stored during three years in a fenced urban yard prior to being sparked by the long ride to this hayfield. His delighted laughter is echoed by that of his young parents watching him exercise his first real taste of freedom. There is no need to call him back or restrain him. His chubby legs will run down long before he runs out of hay. Finally when he can run no more, he flops down in the field still laughing as his father comes to retrieve him.

~

At the time I was born, our family lived near Osakis, Minnesota. I remember Mother talking about my parents' early years together in Glenwood, also a Minnesota town about halfway between St. Cloud and the South Dakota border. My brother was seven years my senior and had lived there for the first years of his life.

I knew Dad had worked for his father during that time. Grandpa owned a livery stable in Glenwood and also provided baled hay to customers in the surrounding community. In later years, after Grandpa had died and Grandma came for summer visits, I heard her conversations with Mother about cooking for the hired men who made up Grandpa's haying crews. Listening to them, I imagined the crew at Grandma's long table consuming mountains of chicken and dumplings, ham, potatoes and gravy, homemade pies, and breads, accompanied by pitchers of milk and pots of strong coffee. It must have been very hot work, I thought, preparing food all morning to serve those huge meals in the midday heat.

As I heard my brother's story, I began to learn how wrong my understanding of Grandpa's haying business had been. I discovered that Grandpa bid on entire hay crops of local farmers and brought his own crews to cut and bale the hay. He then delivered the baled hay to customers who had purchased it directly from him. The noon meal for the crews was prepared in a cookwagon moving during the haying season from farm to farm. The crews went home each night, but the wagon remained. My mother did the cooking and Dad worked with the crew. The cookwagon was their home during haying season.

It was Jerry's first recollection of the hayfields that he had described to me. I thought of the contrast between my brother's free-ranging summer and Mother's confinement in a wagon cooking on a kerosene-fueled stove. My previous conception of mornings spent cooking in a hot farm kitchen suddenly seemed luxurious by comparison. From Jerry's perspective, I could understand that a summer traveling the countryside in a wagon fitted for cooking and sleeping might offer a gypsy-like appeal. For Mother it must have been difficult to attach any sense of adventure to haying season. Yet, as I recall, her comments dealt only with the predominately German foods she prepared for the crew in the blistering heat. It was the preferred and expected fare in a community heavily populated by Germans. Mother's people were Norwegian and she was inclined to view the hearty German dishes with some disdain.

"Too heavy," she sniffed.

Perhaps her stoic Scandinavian reticence kept her from commenting further on conditions of her life that she felt powerless to change.

She enjoyed a reprieve from this annual sojourn to the hayfields when my sister was born in March of 1930. Though Dad continued to work for his father, Mother's cookwagon days were over, and Jerry was presented with the challenge of sharing her attention with the new addition to their household.

❧

The Blueberry Hazard

One of my earliest memories of summer is berry picking with Jerry and Wanda. Our rural Long Prairie, Minnesota location was blessed with ideal growing conditions of soil and climate. We discovered Juneberries, chokecherries, and raspberries growing wild around the edge of the woods, and a lush blueberry patch in a rocky clearing within shouting distance of our house. I liked blueberry picking the best because the berries grew close to the ground making them easy for a small child to find.

On a day filled with sunshine while Jerry and Wanda were busy with chores, I begged Mother to let me go to the blueberry patch. Not surprisingly, her answer was, "Wait for Jerry and Wanda to finish their work, and one of them can take you."

At age four, I was tired of being bossed by my siblings, and continued to wheedle, "Pull-e ease, I know the way."

Mother finally gave in, so I ran to the shed for my berry pail which had been a Karo Syrup container in its previous life, and was out the back door before she could change her mind. Had I known what was in store for me as I marched confidently off to the berry patch, I would not have been so eager.

Oh, the blueberries were lovely, plump and sun-warmed, but I ate only a few. I wanted to bring home enough for Mother to make a pie, or at least muffins. When I returned, Mother was relieved to have me back in her sight and pleased with the berries, but that was before the itching began. Within a few hours my arms, legs, hands, and feet were red and beginning to itch fiercely. There was poison ivy around the berry patch, and without the older children to keep me away from it, my four year old mind was focused only on my mission and didn't give a thought to poison ivy.

On the hot summer nights that followed I tried desperately to sleep and not spread the firey rash any further by scratching, but it was impossible. Mother was fearful of infection as huge blisters appeared on the palms of my hands and the soles of my feet. I knew it was serious when Mother and Daddy took me into Long Prairie to consult a doctor. Doctor visits were rare in our experience. The visit was a disappointment; only calamine lotion was available to help soothe the itching.

Friends and neighbors were consulted for advice, and at one point Daddy went off to the woods to seek out a certain weed a neighbor claimed would provide a cure. The weed was to be boiled and the liquid applied to the rash. Mother boiled up the weeds, producing a nasty-smelling red juice, which did nothing but make me look even worse than I did before the treatment; my blistered arms and legs now streaked and stained with the noxious-smelling red liquid.

Mother kept bandages on my feet because I couldn't bear to wear socks and shoes. It was painful to walk and I found a fallen tree limb to lean on as a crutch of sorts, causing my sister to laughingly comment that I looked like Tiny Tim.

The arrival of my rescuing hero was not on a white charger, but in a Model A Ford. He was the Watkins Man with his assortment of extracts, nectars, spices, *and* patent medicines. Mother spotted a tall yellow cardboard can with a sprinkler top labeled in red block letters, *Watkins Antiseptic Powder.* The word "antiseptic" leaped out at Mother and, being assured by the Watkins Man that it would certainly be effective in battling poison ivy, she bought it without hesitation.

He was barely out of the yard when Mother began the first treatment, sprinkling me liberally with the white powder. It felt soothing, and soon the itching began to subside. Within a few days it was apparent the rash was departing. Perhaps the plague had run its course, and would have cleared without the powder, but nothing would convince Mother of that. The Watkins Man was a hero, and in her mind the antiseptic powder was akin to a magic elixir.

The yellow can with its red lettering reposed in the medicine chest as long as I can remember. It was never, to my knowledge, used again, but the fading, battered yellow cylinder remained on the shelf in the event that we should ever again be desperate enough to resort to this miracle cure.

Alma Pauline Heieie

No writing of Aunt Alma's went unsigned, whether it was a letter, a notation, or a recipe. She signed them "Alma Pauline Heieie, Alma P. Heieie," or occasionally, "A.P.H." This definitive action made me feel she was available to stand by any statement coming from her pen, or should one of her recipes fail, she'd be ready to consult and help determine what went wrong. Her expertise in the art of cooking was largely responsible for providing the funds required to accomplish the goals she had set early in her life. I fell heir to most of her recipes, many of them handwritten and collected in loose leaf binders, each with the familiar scrawled signature.

I discovered that she often jotted notes in the margins of these cookbooks, sometimes expressing a thought she wanted to record before it escaped her, or perhaps a notation about a family event. I never knew when I would come upon these bits of marginalia, so cooking with her recipes not only produced delightful results, but assumed the quality of a visit with this favorite aunt.

In thirty years of baking, I had not turned out a loaf of white bread to my liking until I used Aunt Alma's recipe. It was not so different from those I had used in the past, but it was as if she stood behind me encouraging and smiling approvingly as I kneaded the fragrant dough. What nonsense, I thought, but there were the firm light, heavenly smelling loaves of white bread cooling on the rack. A few years had passed since she left this earth, but she was still making an impact. Despite the fact that some of the recipes were hastily scrawled, the writing faded and difficult to read, I have not rewritten them lest it would somehow spoil the magic.

Alma, born September 11, 1894, was the fourth child of Randi and Gunnilius Heieie. A Homestead Certificate filed in 1906 at the Land Office in Crookston, Minnesota verified a claim of Gunnilius O. Heieie for one hundred and sixty acres of land. The family farmed that land until Aunt Alma bought a home for her parents in Monticello, Minnesota after the children were grown.

Alma would have four more sisters before a boy (the ninth child) was born. My mother was one of the younger sisters. By the time their brother, Marion, was welcomed into the family, Alma had made plans. She was good looking and intelligent, strong in her religious faith, and practical. Alma was determined that she would see to her sisters' schooling, not only in domestic skills, but in the Three R's as well. She managed to accomplish this, though not always with their gratitude as they were not all as industrious as Alma and considered her "bossy." Her plan for Marion was to provide tuition funding so he could attend the University of Minnesota in preparation for a professional career.

When she had completed the eighth grade (as far as the country school could take her) she looked for an opportunity to work for room and board while she attended high school. She found such an opportunity at Badger, Minnesota and tells about high school graduation in the following excerpt from her journal:

> Olette and Hannah came and stayed at Larson's overnight, the only two from home that could make it for the graduation. Each graduate had to write an essay on some person or subject. Miss Reed, our principal, had given us a list from which we could choose. I chose Joan of Arc, not knowing at that time of our "French" background in our father's mother's father who was an officer in the French army during Napoleon's reign. He was one of a few men selected to be sent up in a balloon for exploration, which landed in northern Norway. Those men never returned to France having decided they had had enough of Napoleon's wars. Great Grandfather married, lived and died in Norway.

~

I must digress a moment here to comment on the balloonist. My mother had an aversion to this story, and was visibly dismayed when Aunt Alma let the cat out of the bag by referring to it in our hearing, without taking the precaution of lapsing into Norwegian (as they usually did when they deemed the conversation unsuitable for childish ears). Mother cautioned us not to mention it to anyone as there may be "repercussions" considering our ancestor was actually a deserter from the French army.

Privately, my sister and I would ask each other, "Does she expect us to believe they're still looking for him?"

This would send us into peals of laughter as we saw through the thinly veiled attempt to deny that any but pure Norwegian blood could have found its way into her family. Aunt Alma, on the other hand, was inclined to accept the fact of the sullied bloodline with her usual equanimity. We found the whole thing particularly amusing since Mother had chosen a person of French background to be her children's father.

Following graduation, Alma moved on to further her education as related in her journal:

1911—Hannah and I attended teachers training school at Roseau, Minnesota. We stayed at Wold's (twelve girls rooming there). While we were there, our brother-in-law, John, came and gave us a ride to Pencer to see our sister, Claudina, and her first baby, Julian.... Returning to school in 1912, I was alone as Hannah had been married in June. I had my eighteenth birthday on September 11, 1912.

$\sim$

Alma received her teaching certificate and taught for two years before setting out for Superior, Wisconsin, where a cousin, Edwin Thompson, owned a store. She could work there to earn her keep while she attended the "New Era Business College." There she became adept at operation of the typewriter and stenotype (a machine that recorded symbols in shorthand for later transcription).

After completing this course, she returned home and accepted a summer job in a hotel kitchen to put aside enough money to begin seeking a permanent position. Asked if she could bake bread, she replied in the affirmative, and this marked the end of her teaching days and stenotype operation. Her journal states:

I had my dear mother to thank for her good bread and for her patiently teaching us all to become good cooks.

~

After the bread, it was discovered that she was equally adept at turning out other baked goods of excellent quality, as well as fine cooking. She apparently had the capacity to manage mass food preparation (not surprising when one considers the size of the family in which her skills were acquired). She soon discovered these skills were very much in demand, thereby providing her with a far better income than teaching or stenography offered.

By the time I was born in 1933, Aunt Alma was nearly forty years old, and managing a home at White Bear Lake for a member of the James Hill family. She had already purchased a home for her parents, and Uncle Marion was at the University of Minnesota enrolled in pre-med, studying for a degree in dentistry.

Alma had not married, and remained single the rest of her life. I don't believe she allowed herself to consider marriage as an option; she needed all the energy she possessed to carry out her plans for the family. Marriage was hard on country women in the early part of the century. Both Claudina and Hannah had died long before I was born. Aunt Olette had lost her fiance in the first World War and never married. Alma engaged her assistance to complete Marion's education. The shy Olette was happy to help out, and though her income was modest, she quietly managed the home they shared, allowing Alma to focus her energy on family business.

My earliest memories of Alma, Olette, and Marion are of their visits to our home near Long Prairie at Christmas and during the summer. A Chrysler Town and Country wagon was made available to Alma by her employer. She did not drive, so Marion was at the wheel. This was a vehicle beyond our dreams with its polished wood panels and roomy interior. Out of that big wagon came presents, new clothes, and a wealth of Alma's special foods and baked goods. These dear aunts and uncle treated us as if we were their own, and we basked in the unaccustomed pampering.

Over the years, they continued to visit us and were a special part of holidays and summer picnics. After Marion's marriage, his wife, LaFaye, accompanied him on his visits. Through them, I came to realize the importance to young people of the genuine interest and unconditional acceptance by adults other than their parents.

Years later, when I had children of my own, these memories suggested to me that it would be nice to write each of them a letter telling them how important they had been to me throughout my life and how much they meant to me. I am grateful for the inspiration that prompted me to write those letters.

My parents celebrated their Golden Wedding Anniversary at their home in Minneapolis on February 14, 1971. It was the last time I was to see Aunt Alma. She was living in a Minneapolis apartment after selling her Wayzata home following the death of Olette a few years earlier. In the course of our visit, she quietly observed that this may be the last time we would all be together. She was smiling, and did not seem dismayed by the prospect. I felt hot tears well up, but Aunt Alma said, "Oh my! Now that is nothing to cry about; it's perfectly normal for life to move along. We've always had such lovely times together."

It was so simple and matter-of-fact the way she spelled it out, and I swallowed my tears. I was sure she was preparing me for her taking leave of us, yet somehow she made it seem all right. She was now eighty, had worked hard, and accomplished her goals.

When I received word of Aunt Alma's death a short time later, I was not surprised and her reassuring words during our last visit came back to me, transcending my grief. I do not feel she ever left me. She is with me in my kitchen speaking to me through her writing as I consult the magic recipes signed with a flourish, "Alma P. Heieie."

∿

The Constitution
and the Boll Eyes

My earliest memories include solitary hours spent playing in the yard while Mother tended to indoor chores and cared for my baby sister. I was two when Vonnie was born in 1935. Our other two siblings, Jerry and Wanda were in school most of the year. Isolation was an accepted element of rural Minnesota life, particularly in winter. This was felt in varying degrees depending on the size of your family, the proximity of nearest neighbors, the size of their family, and availability of transportation.

It would have been difficult to be an only child in that time and place unless there were neighbor children nearby to offer some companionship. Playmates might provide an opportunity to experience the negotiations that siblings constantly employ in forming associations and partnerships among themselves as part of their socialization.

In winter we could count on plenty of blowing and drifting snow to make driving difficult. We had one car which was not always cooperative on the coldest days, even with old woolen quilts piled on the hood overnight. Often confined to the house by cold weather, we were grateful (as was Mother) for the days we could go sliding, our favorite winter activity.

We had a great hill for this purpose, despite the generally flat terrain of the area. The hill began just beyond our driveway on the sparsely traveled county road. With running starts and belly flops onto our sleds, we picked up momentum quickly on the long, curving slope for exhilarating rides. It was well worth the walk back uphill pulling our sleds, with exhaled breath appearing in clouds that frosted the edges of our hand-knit wool scarves.

Summer meant freedom for me. Jerry and Wanda were out of school and I tagged along with them to discover the natural wonders beyond the grove of trees at the edge of our property. We picked berries and explored the pond where we collected frogs and tadpoles.

When I reached school age, my boredom and loneliness were relieved. My confinement to the yard was eased, and the school experience prepared me to hold my own better with Jerry and Wanda. The Kardash family, with children our ages, lived within a mile of our home and we occasionally played together. But the Kardash children had little free time as they were required to help care for a number of farm animals.

Toys were not plentiful in the country homes of the thirties. We were dependent on our own imaginations for much of our entertainment. When inclement weather kept us in the house, we often consulted the Sears Roebuck catalogue for inspiration. We pored over the toy section admiring the shiny bikes and Betsy-Wetsy dolls (which drank from tiny baby bottles and wet their diapers). How we envied the lucky kids who found these items under their Christmas trees! We usually paused a guilty moment to inspect and snicker over the underwear pages where brazen models paraded immodestly in nothing but their underwear for all the world to see.

Jerry and Wanda had been rivals since the day her birth interrupted his sole claim on our parents' attention. Years later, in a dinner table declaration one evening, he even proclaimed her to be "The Cause of All His Troubles." They co-existed in uneasy periods of truce. Breaks in those periods present-ed me with opportunities to team up with Jerry for short spells of respite from his typical big-brother teasing.

On one of these occasions, he recruited me to join forces with him and form a secret club. Still smarting from a falling-out with Wanda, I didn't hes-itate to sign on. I was intrigued with his suggestion and flattered that he would bother with a seven year old. Undaunted, Wanda enlisted Vonnie to join up with her and form their own secret club. There was no question of selection of presidents in these organizations. My president informed me that our primary mission would be to spy on Wanda and Vonnie, and we began by lurking in the hall to eavesdrop as President Wanda laid out their plans. We smirked scornfully when we heard her say, "We'll start by writing down the Constitution and the Bylaws."

The clueless five year old Vonnie innocently inquired of her big sister, "What's the Constitution and the Boll Eyes?"

Our smirking turned to guffaws, revealing our intrusion on their business meeting amid cries of "No Fair!" from Wanda. Jerry was unmerciful in his taunts.

"Some club you've got. Your member can't even say 'bylaws,' much less read them."

It didn't occur to Jerry that I was questioning in my mind why *Our Club* didn't have a Constitution and Bylaws. Wanda seemed to know what she was doing, and I was already considering defecting and transferring my membership to her club. Perhaps it *had* occurred to him, and his scornful laughter was employed to cover the fact that he lacked certain organizational skills.

The clubs were disbanded by silent, mutual consent with a little intervention by Mother when she discovered that we two younger children were being used as pawns in the ongoing rivalry between Jerry and Wanda.

Today, the mention of the constitution and the boll eyes unfailingly conjures up memories of childhood that reach far beyond those of the secret clubs.

∾

The School
at Lake Beauty

On a bright September day in 1939, just before my sixth birthday, I eagerly set off to begin first grade. There was no kindergarten at Lake Beauty School, so this was the first day of the next two and a half years I would spend there. The school was located two miles from our home near Long Prairie and I followed my eighth grade brother, Jerry and my sister, Wanda, who was starting fifth grade, as they took shortcuts through fields and pastures.

I was a little apprehensive, remembering my visit at school last spring. Students were allowed to bring five-year-old siblings for a day-long visit near the end of the school year; sort of a 1938 version of orientation later known as "round-up" in my children's educational system. During my spring visit I forgot the "no talking" rule and burst out with, "Let it go wa-a-a-y down!" as Wanda was demonstrating the globe on a pulley that raised it out of the way when not in use. I was mortified by the teacher's frown and admonition to my sister to *keep me quiet.* To my chagrin, Wanda related the incident at the dinner table with great emphasis on her embarrassment over my bad behavior. I was relieved to learn that Lake Beauty had a new teacher this year. I could start school with a clean slate.

I was armed with knowledge of the alphabet and numbers (acquired while "playing school" with Wanda) but longed to learn to read for myself. The woman who was to undertake the task of teaching me, along with seven other grades of students, was Miss Classman, whose family owned the photography studio in Long Prairie. I never knew her first name and did not presume to ask anyone. I adored her. She was twenty one years old, tall, slim, blond, and beautiful. Her stern demeanor seemed appropriate for someone carrying her heavy responsibilities. I realize now that she was not much older than some of the eighth grade boys, and certainly not much bigger. It was imperative for her to gain the upper hand and maintain it with this half-dozen eighth graders, the largest class in school.

Lake Beauty School, a neat white-painted wooden building, stood alone on a gravel surfaced county road. The interior consisted of one main room with a cloak hall and a small alcove that served as a library. A washroom with a chemical toilet completed the accommodations. Heat was supplied by a wood burning stove, valiantly striving to hold at bay the bitter cold of Minnesota winters. Fingers of icy air reached from the drafty building's windows and far corners where the stove failed to radiate its heat. Layers of warm clothing were required to protect us from drafts as we worked at our wrought iron desks with well-worn oak tops.

I wore woolen sweaters over my dresses and much hated tan, cotton stockings pulled over long underwear producing an unattractive lumpy-legged appearance. Our heavy wool snowpants and coats hung damply from their cloakroom hooks. As the snow we had picked up on our trek through fields and frozen swamps began to melt, the smell of wet wool quickly permeated the building on winter mornings. Our hats reposed with lunch pails on the shelf above our respective hooks, and the ugly, but practical buckle overshoes stood in little puddles on the floor beneath them. For headwear, most of the girls favored the parka hood, a knitted woolen hat that reached down the back of the neck; wide ties in front served as a scarf. Aviator helmets of leather (some with goggles, ala Charles Lindbergh) were popular with the boys.

A part-time custodian supplied cut wood to fuel the stove, shoveled snow, and took care of cleaning the premises. The teacher arrived early in the morning to start the fire, which she maintained during the day with assistance from the older boys.

In front of the classroom, a raised platform with blackboards stretching across the wall behind it, held the teacher's desk and chair. This platform doubled as a stage for presentations of plays and holiday programs. On those occasions, curtains were hung by hooks from a rod, allowing them to be pulled back (by hand, of course) to reveal the petrified performers on stage.

As the only student in my class, I received Miss Classman's undivided attention during the time allotted for first grade teaching. This, coupled with my desire to learn, resulted in rapid progress and to my delight, I was soon reading by myself the stories of Dick, Jane, and their dog Spot. It was the first time in my life that I had received this kind of concentrated attention.

Unlike the classroom, recess and lunch were times to be simply endured. Shy, and the youngest child in school, I was intimidated by the older children. I tried to avoid their attention (and hence their teasing scorn) on the unsupervised playground. I was secretly pleased on the rare occasions when bad weather kept us inside for lunch and recess. Whenever possible, I volunteered to clap erasers or wash blackboards so I could remain inside with Miss Classman. I couldn't get by with this often, as she believed it was important for children to get outside for fresh air and exercise during the school day. It also elicited announcements by Jerry at the dinner table that I was teacher's pet, and worse, that I was using the ruse of offering the teacher my help to maintain that status.

As Christmas neared, a festive evening was planned with Santa Claus, treats, and entertainment for the parents. This presentation heralded my first stage appearance. Music instruction at Lake Beauty included all classes and consisted of singing from *The Golden Book of Song.* During class it was observed that Wanda and I could sing on key, and when she informed Miss Classman that we could also sing in harmony, we became the main attraction of the Christmas carol presentation. From the time I began singing, our mother had taught us to harmonize, but to this point our audience had been only family. I was horrified at the prospect of being singled out for exposure to more ridicule from the "Big Kids." When Wanda told Mother about our part in the program, Mother declared that we must have new outfits and set about sewing pretty red dresses in keeping with the season. At night after we had gone to bed, I would hear her at the treadle sewing machine working to finish the new finery on time. Meanwhile, Wanda and I practiced diligently.

The big evening finally arrived, and the family set off in the car with great excitement. Too soon it was our turn to sing. I was fairly paralyzed by stage fright, but clutching my hand, Wanda dragged me out on the stage behind the curtains which were opened by the students entrusted with this key assignment. At the sound of Miss Classman's pitch pipe, I felt Wanda squeeze my hand (our signal to begin). Miraculously, I found I could breathe and sing as we quavered into the opening strains of "Silent Night." We knew all the practice had paid off when we heard the enthusiastic applause of our classmates and their families.

Following the carols, there were readings and recitations of poetry. Names had been drawn for an exchange of small gifts. Refreshments topped off the evening. It was a heady feeling for the youngest kid at school to reap the praise and approval of teacher, parents, and even some of the older students. I considered the evening a huge success.

Spring came, and with it graduation day for the eighth graders, who would begin high school in the fall at the small town of Swanville. The next year Jerry would be taking the bus to school, and wouldn't have a chance to torment me in second grade. He recently told me that throughout eighth grade he had disliked Miss Classman intensely. Then she spoke to each of her eighth graders before graduation, telling them she may have been strict, but it was only because she wanted so much for them to be the best they could be. In retrospect, he considered her the best teacher he had ever had.

Miss Classman was not at Lake Beauty the next year and, although I liked her replacement, Miss Neiwahner, no one could measure up to Miss Classman in my eyes. In second grade, I was again the lone child in my class, and had the teacher's full attention.

As a second grader, I worked with the older students on penmanship using lined paper with steel-tipped wooden pens dipped into glass inkwells inserted in holes at the upper right corner of our desks. The teacher filled these inkwells with an interesting squeeze-bottle device sporting a rubber nozzle designed to prevent dripping. Girls with long braids were often subjected to having the ends of their hair dipped in inkwells by the boys seated behind them. I was glad I didn't have braids. We managed to get our fingers liberally ink-smeared during penmanship, as we struggled to keep up with the teacher's chant of, "Oval, oval, oval, compact oval."

The idea of this was to help develop a rhythm and a free-flowing hand as we tried to form perfect ovals of exactly the same size. In addition to "compact" ovals, we practiced lines of ovals that rolled out like corkscrews across the page.

We also worked at grammar and spelling in combined grades to some extent so I was learning sentence structure and other more difficult exercises that were introduced to me as new material later in city schools. I found this to be the case with math as well. The small classes allowed for intensified individual instruction, which prepared us well to work with larger classes in years to come.

I continued to advance rapidly in reading with encouragement from the teacher, and read far beyond second grade level. This scored me a starring role in the planned Thanksgiving pageant. The teacher assigned me the job of narrating several pages of Longfellow's *Song of Hiawatha* while selected students dressed as pilgrims and Indians enacted the story of the first Thanksgiving on the stage behind me. I took this honor seriously, so when I realized, after taking home my copy of the poem printed out on sheets of tablet paper by the teacher, I hadn't asked if I was to memorize the poem or read it. I had the whole weekend before me, so to be on the safe side, I memorized it.

At rehearsal time, I asked the teacher if I was "supposed to look at my paper." She looked at me skeptically and asked if I could recite it without the paper. I assured her I could, and she said, "Well, we can try it."

By then I was a seasoned performer (having the Christmas party experience under my belt) and I did my recitation without help from the prompter installed behind the curtain as a precautionary measure.

I cite these small triumphs to illustrate the extent of the time and effort invested by those teachers in the rural schools of my childhood. In spite of limited resources, they unfailingly sought ways to spark an interest in art and music, without losing sight of the need for a strong foundation of basic skills. They captured our imaginations, and motivated us to achievements that surprised us.

In the middle of the third grade we moved to Long Prairie, where the school building housed high school, as well as grades one through eight and seemed enormous. Certainly, we had the advantage of walking a few blocks

on sidewalks instead of the long hike to Lake Beauty. I was thrilled to discover the Long Prairie Library and quickly made friends with the librarian.
I liked my teachers and having classmates of my own age, but I recall no
other elementary school experience with the same appreciation as I remember those first years at Lake Beauty.

Fall From Grace

*R*ural Minnesota in the 1930s offered an active child of seven a world of freedom and wholesome home-grown food. In spite of the country being in the throes of economic depression, we felt safe, and best of all, we could run into the house at any time and find our mother there. Jerry was fourteen, Wanda ten, and our sister Vonnie was five.

Providing for our needs occupied all of Mother's waking hours and we were each required to assume some of the household chores appropriate to our ages. Beyond that, we were expected to do our homework, entertain ourselves when not in school, and Stay Out of Trouble.

Oh, the lovely sense of freedom when, chores and homework completed, we could escape to the outdoors. It was peacefully quiet with wide open spaces for games and virtually no traffic on the country road where we lived. The extent of our adventures was limited only by the scope of our imaginations, certainly not hampered by an abundance of slick toys. New toys were about as scarce as playmates. The nearest neighbor with children lived close to a mile down the road. Mostly, we depended on one another for company. It was a peaceful and simple existence, but shortly after my second year of school began, my small world was to be invaded by a cloud of shame that I looked upon in later years as my Fall From Grace.

Mother had received rigid religious training in her Norwegian Lutheran family, heavily influenced by a couple of stern-faced uncles who were preachers. Mercifully, we had seen them only in photos glaring their disapproval from the pages of Mother's album. Her years of exposure to their hell-fire and brimstone preaching had endowed Mother with a grave concern for the salvation of our souls and she insisted that we be provided with the same strict teaching she had received. My quick temper and feisty attitude seemed to thwart my best efforts to measure up to Mother's (and I was sure God's) expectations. I was painfully aware of my shortcomings and by age seven had managed to burden myself with quite a hefty load of guilt to which I was about to make a sizable addition.

Relying as we did on one another for playmates, we had our share of squabbles. As the third child in the family, I was constantly seeking the acceptance and approval of my older brother and sister. I found I could often score a playmate by taking advantage of the rivalry between them. Jerry's resentment toward Wanda for being born, thus ending his only-child position, remained close to the surface and flared up with some regularity. At those times, I would (if only by default) gain a temporary ally.

My Fall From Grace was sparked by my discovery of Wanda's hiding place for her diary. Knowing Jerry would love to have this information, I attempted to ingratiate myself to him by divulging the secret location. What an opportunity, I thought, to retaliate for all the suffering (real or imagined) I had endured at Wanda's hands. At the same time, I was sure to enjoy a long spell of Jerry's favor.

For a few heady hours I was on a little power trip basking in the glow of big-brother approval. It all ended abruptly when the family gathered for dinner and a mocking falsetto voice from my brother's place at the table piped, "I think I'm falling for Harry!"

I did not need to see the look of disbelief on Wanda's face to figure out the source of that line. Harry was a member of Wanda's sixth grade class in the one-room school we all attended. A week earlier Harry had fainted in class after he accidentally stabbed himself in the hand while fooling around with his compass. The mishap resulted in Wanda's first school-girl crush, inspired by compassion and confided only to her diary.

The revelation and the diabolical means of delivery had the desired effect. It took only a glance at my crestfallen face to identify the guilty party. I was rewarded with appropriate disdain and anger communicated by a look of pure hatred directed at me from Wanda. Mother's eyes conveyed her disappointment as she reminded me that it was not a nice thing to do. Dad cautioned Jerry not to mention it at school. Beyond that, my parents, surprisingly, seemed to view the incident as kid stuff. I'm sure, however, with the insight lacking in a seven year old, they knew I had dug myself a pretty deep hole and would live to regret my betrayal. It all seemed to blow over quickly, but my misery was just beginning. I didn't even want to think about what those harsh uncles in Mother's album (not to mention God) would have to say about this!

I knew I had broken the Golden Rule, and I squirmed as I pictured myself in Wanda's place as the one humiliated in front of the whole family. I agonized and rationalized. It wasn't a huge betrayal. I had just seen her put the diary there; she hadn't actually told me the hiding place. Therefore, I didn't think I deserved to be ranked with a Judas. Hadn't Wanda hurt me plenty of times? And, yes, Jerry too had more than once been subjected to her scornful ridicule.

I finally admitted to myself that I had behaved badly, selling out to gain favor with someone who, more often than not, represented the common enemy in our small world.

∾

Calamity on the Hill Road

To a child of six, the hill seemed enormous, more mountain than hill. Our rural Minnesota home sat at the very top of the "hill road," as it was known around Todd County. The gravel road curved around a wooded bend that always appeared cold and dark, even on the brightest summer day. A huge grey rock in the foreground was in constant shadow cast by the dense foliage around it, which presented an ominous appearance to my impressionable mind.

Nevertheless, when snow fell, no child could ask for a better sliding hill. As I cruised around the bend, I studiously ignored the big rock, even though the contrast between warm sunshine and cold darkness, so apparent in summer, was not evident with the foliage gone and soft snow covering the landscape.

On a bitter January day in 1939 a car came chugging up the hill road and turned into our driveway. I ran to clear a space on the frosted living room window and get a peek at who was brave enough to venture out in such cold weather. I was delighted to see our neighbors, the Cashes, with their children emerging from the car. They had no more entered the house than Tootsie, one of the daughters, suggested sliding on the hill road. Four year old Vonnie immediately began clamoring to go with us.

"She'll just cry because it's too cold," I told Mother.

But Vonnie, as usual, prevailed. So with a sigh of resignation, I stuffed her into her furry brown coat and pulled on her boots. I was envious of the coat, wishing the well-heeled cousin who had outgrown it had been bigger so I could have been the lucky recipient of the hand-me-down. As always, the envy as well as resentment at having to take her with us, was tempered by protective love for the baby of the family.

There were not enough sleds to go around, so we were required to share. There were two sleds available for the three of us that day, but we did have a clumsy homemade wooden sled with a handle for pushing which my brother used to haul wood. Tootsie suggested we use that clumsy sled which could carry two of us with the third person pushing. She offered to take the first turn pushing, so we put Vonnie in the sled and headed down the driveway.

At the top of the hill road, I settled Vonnie in the sled and climbed on board. Tootsie pushed off struggling to control the crude, heavy sled with no turning capacity. She was able to hold on for only a few seconds of our descent before she was left stumbling along the crest of the hill. As we approached the curve, the roadside snowbank loomed before us and I realized there was no way I could turn the sled to follow the curve. We slammed into the snowbank, and while we were picking ourselves up, Tootsie had run down the hill and was capering around the disaster scene.

"Why did you let go?" I shouted angrily.

Now standing in the road, a spidery little figure with arms akimbo, the crestfallen Tootsie certainly didn't look capable of controlling the heavy sled. Vonnie was crying and complaining that her arm hurt, so we loaded her on the sled and together pushed her back up the hill and home.

I was feeling pretty scared and guilty, knowing that I had failed to take proper care of Vonnie. As she was getting Vonnie unbundled, Mother was scolding me for taking the big sled. If I had asked, I would have been told how dangerous it was and avoided the accident. Suddenly Mother stopped scolding as she took off the furry coat to discover one chubby arm hanging limp and useless with a lump appearing on the forearm. She was close to fainting as she called in a choked voice for Dad to come and help. They carefully wrapped Vonnie in a blanket, and the older children were left in charge while the adults took her to Long Prairie for medical attention. Mother and Dad had no time to explain or speculate about treatment as they rushed off, so we had no idea what would be done for a broken bone. The older children spoke of splints and slings, but none of us had ever known anyone with a broken bone.

While we waited with trepidation, we selected some favorite items from our meager horde of treasured possessions—an empty perfume bottle, a satin ribbon, a well-worn picture book—to give to the small invalid.

When she returned sporting a heavy plaster cast, we were appalled, but our dismay turned to amazement at her resourcefulness in adjusting to the use of only one arm. After announcing, to our envy, that the doctor had given her a dime for being such a good girl, she was put to bed to rest from her ordeal where we presented her with our lavish gifts. The perfume bottle was her favorite, and immediately went between little toes to hold it so she could remove the cover with her free hand in the hope that a trace of fragrance might remain inside.

As everyone exclaimed how clever she was, and she basked in the unaccustomed attention and gifts, the guilt I suffered for letting such a calamity befall "The Baby" was suddenly invaded by a twinge of envy. All this and a dime besides! But looking at that sweet face, I could begrudge her nothing. After all, she was our precious little sister.

❧

Why Does Everything Happen to Vonnie?

*Y*vonne, or Vonnie as we call her, is the baby of our family, and as children we called her "Baby" or "The Baby" until she protested loudly at age four, "I am not a baby, my name is Yvonne!"

She had made her point, and we finally ceased the demeaning address, but that did not deter us from continuing to baby her. She was cute, and so vulnerable that we all felt she needed special protection. Additionally, the ills that invaded our family, though rare, usually targeted Vonnie.

"Everything Happens to Vonnie," we cried in protest each time a small mishap, serious illness, or accident occurred.

In her second winter she was stricken with pneumonia, and Wanda and I cowered by the woodbox next to the cookstove in the kitchen while the doctor tended her into the night.

Terrified she would die, we were afraid to stay up and afraid that if we went to bed we'd find her gone in the morning.

Bronchial problems continued to plague her, and the small chest was frequently swaddled in evil smelling mustard plasters concocted of dry mustard and hot water between layers of flannel. I was wracked with guilt when she suffered a broken arm under my care sliding on the "hill road."

She had a tendency to dawdle and in later years after we moved to Duluth, I would sometimes go to school without her to avoid being late myself. I'd lie to her teacher when asked where Vonnie was.

"Oh, she didn't feel well," I'd say. Then after Vonnie strolled in, I would be reprimanded by her teacher as I scrambled to cover my lie by saying, "I guess she must have started to feel better after I left home."

Our winter walks to school were delayed by Vonnie stopping in her tracks and sniffling as she complained that her hands were cold. The only way I could remedy that was to remove my wool mittens and pull them on over hers, jam my hands in my coat pockets, and try to hurry her along. We lived only three blocks from school.

I couldn't figure out how she managed to get her stockings so grubby (often out at the knees) during recess. More than once her teacher, Miss MacDonald, summoned me to her room after school to point this out to me and suggest that I correct the unfortunate tendency in my younger sibling. She studiously ignored my protests that I didn't share Vonnie's recess period, and so could not watch over her on the playground. I resented her admonitions to me that it wasn't fair to come home with torn and dirty stockings for my "poor mother" to mend and wash. Anyway, I didn't see how it made much difference what happened to the ugly long brown cotton stockings we wore during the cold months (which was most of the school year in Duluth).

The most bizarre dilemma to befall Vonnie occurred on the Fourth of July in 1938 when I was five years old, a few years before our move to Duluth. It was not serious, but reinforced our claim that indeed, Everything Happened to Vonnie. I call this incident the "Fireworks After the Fireworks."

It didn't take a lot of excitement to make a day special, living as we did in a rural area where nothing out of the ordinary happened most days of the year. I awoke early that morning, drawn quickly to the kitchen by the aroma of frying chicken. I found Mother at the stove stirring home cooked dressing for the potato salad she was preparing for our favorite picnic lunch. She assured me that she had put aside some potato salad with no eggs for me. It was a time-consuming task to prepare the Fourth of July picnic which she would serve on the shore of Lake Osakis at noon. But busy as she was, Mother took extra time to cater to my finicky appetite. The baked beans had been started the night before. A devils food cake would top off the feast. After lunch we would take turns in the boat with daddy fishing for crappies and sunfish.

It was a perfect summer day, and as we drove to the lake, three small American flags fluttering from each headlight of our Willis Knight car added a special flair to the holiday. The blue field held only forty-eight stars then, as Hawaii and Alaska had not yet been added to the Union.

We were home by late afternoon to size up our supply of firecrackers, cap guns and caps, and the sparklers which would not be lit until evening. Meanwhile we contented ourselves with playing cowboys, delighted with the luxury of real ammunition to blast off instead of yelling, "Bang! Bang!"

After dark we capered around the yard waving our sparklers, and when they were all spent, we chased fireflies (we called them lightening bugs) with Mason jars borrowed from Mother's pantry. Somehow we remembered to place the hot, sharp wires from the sparklers in the designated spot instead of dropping them in the yard in our excitement. We were thus spared burning our bare feet or piercing them with the wires.

It was after we returned to the house that Vonnie's strangled cries brought us running to the living room. Mother's sewing basket was open and in disarray where it sat with its endless supply of mending on a table near her chair. Vonnie had been exploring the contents and found a small triangular tool designed to slip over the ends of flat curtain rods to allow lace curtains to be threaded over the rough metal. It was slippery and shiny, and for unknown reasons, Vonnie decided it would just fit her tongue. Once the tongue was inserted, the curtain threader hung on as an appendage and refused to let go. Vonnie's efforts to free herself had only resulted in the swelling and bruising of her tongue.

Daddy applied his usual remedy—shouting that we shouldn't have a thing like that around the house for kids to be tempted by—while Mother quietly fetched cold water to see if that might do the trick. With a cool head and cool cloths, Mother coaxed the curtain threader to give up and release its three year old prisoner. Daddy immediately seized the nasty piece of metal, ran to the front door and flung it out into the darkness. Our special day which had begun on such a festive note had suddenly fizzled like a burned-out sparkler. Mother said nothing in response to Daddy's outburst, but quietly herded us off to bed.

The next morning after breakfast when Daddy had left for work, Mother summoned Jerry, Wanda, and me, and led us out to the front yard. Without explanation, she chose a place which she marked and then brought Jerry to the mark, handed him a small stone and instructed him to throw it as hard as he could. She watched the trajectory, walked out, inspected the landing area, and retrieved the stone. She repeated the ritual with me, and then with Wanda. When she inspected the landing area of Wanda's stone she bent twice to pick up two objects, which on her return we discovered to be the stone and the curtain threader.

It was our secret, never to be revealed to our father. Our four-way conspiracy made us feel important, having been entrusted with an adult confidence. Vonnie was oblivious to the purpose of the game, and Mother simply found a new, safe location for the offending tool.

Sometimes my mother was pure magic.

Part Two:

Kneading the Bread

Kay Henderson

*K*ay Henderson was more than a childhood friend. We came to regard her as almost a member of the family. On a day in the late 1930s, when Dad unwittingly brought her home in a bin of scrap paper, we rescued her and thus became responsible for her welfare from that day forward.

The depression still held the nation in its relentless grip, and Dad had discovered he could eke out a few extra dollars by collecting, baling, and selling scrap paper. He collected the paper from business offices and department stores in the small towns around Long Prairie. After hauling it home in his trailer, he sorted and baled it in large rectangles secured with heavy wire. His four children eagerly clamored to help sort out the foreign items that found their way into the paper bins. We uncovered many treasures (especially from the department stores) to add to our meager collections. New clothing, accessories, knick-knacks, and even jewelry appeared among the accounting sheets and discarded wrappings. One of my favorite finds was a paperweight, a miniature replica of the Empire State Building.

We finally located the source of the odd smell that permeated the piles of paper and stubbornly refused to leave some of our treasures. It was a vaguely musty citrus odor that originated in discarded employee lunch bags. Many contained none too fresh orange peels. The federal government, through a relief program offering nutritional supplements to the under-employed, distributed endless crates of oranges, which found their way into the country's lunchbags. If the odor clung to Kay, we didn't notice, enchanted as we were by her elegance.

Certain that I was the first to spot Kay's delicate face among the paper from Henderson's Department Store, I was furious when Wanda, instantly claimed her, beating me to the punch. Kay was a miniature mannequin about two feet in height. Her petite, perfectly proportioned figure was clad in a cunning little undergarment with dainty zipper and tiny hook and eye closings. Kay in her previous life had obviously been a corset model at Henderson's, evidenced by the name *Henderson's* boldly emblazoned across her chest. But what could possibly have caused such an ignominious end to her career?

Wanda gently removed her from the bin, and then we saw it—a blow to the elegant nose had inflicted significant damage. So this was what brought her down from her lofty position atop the corset counter where our goddess had silently enticed the prairie women of Granite Falls, Minnesota, to purchase Henderson's foundation garments in the hope they would transform their figures to match hers.

The sight of the facial injury made me think Mother was right in her admonitions that beauty was only skin deep, and if we relied on it to carry us through life, we would end up alone and lonely when it faded. But we had high hopes of restoring Kay's beauty with a nose job.

Kay was not endowed with real hair, but the plaster coiffure resembling a soft dark cloud was quite satisfactory. Her torso was fashioned like a dressmaker's dummy with no arms, and thighs that disappeared into a square stand designed for stability. The Venus de Milo quality presented a challenge when Wanda began to create a wardrobe for Kay from scraps of mother's precious fabrics. Sleeveless garments were settled on as the best solution.

Selection of this beauty's name warranted serious consideration. Wanda often chose fanciful names for her dolls, like "Cloth Ear Saunders" and "Fancy Fargo," but the glamorous mannequin required a name befitting her dignity. Wanda felt the name "Kay" was elegant sounding and went well with Henderson. (There was no question of the last name, branded as it was on her chest.)

Once the christening was settled, Wanda went to work on the nose with fine sandpaper begged from Dad, an emery board, and a few cosmetics from Mother's modest collection. Her attempted surgical procedure was not entirely successful. The cruel wound was reduced to a dent and camouflaged by makeup, but further bobbing of the nose would have resulted in a snubbed look entirely unsuitable for Kay. So Wanda decided Kay's left side would be her "bad angle," a Hollywood expression I knew she had lifted directly from the pages of *Photoplay* magazine.

Kay displayed her new wardrobe in a corner of the bedroom I shared with my two sisters, where the light was flattering and played up her "good angle." She seemed comfortable enough in our modest surroundings, protected from exposure to the glare of the spotlight.

In 1943, when my father's Minnesota State Guard unit was mobilized following Japan's attack on Pearl Harbor, our world changed drastically. He was sent to Duluth, and we would soon follow him to that city on the shore of Lake Superior. City life would have suited Kay perfectly but alas, Mother had to be relentless about what we could take along and Kay, in spite of her petite figure was too awkward to pack. Unwilling to give up Kay completely, Wanda's solution was drastic, but practical. She planned to decapitate Kay and take the head along. When we reached Duluth, she would use Kay as a "cosmetics model" in a beauty salon. The decapitation, performed with Dad's saw, proved to be a difficult operation. The result was not a clean cut such as a guillotine would have produced. The hacked, lumpy, white plaster protruding from the stump of the long, smooth throat was startling. But worse, the headless torso in its now slightly dingy corset, could have come straight from the lurid page of *True Detective*, a publication featuring real criminal cases. The chalky white substance appearing at the base of the neck between the shoulders was almost more alarming than the sight of blood. Unlike most of the *True Detective* cases, this one ended with a decent burial before Wanda packed up the head for our move to Northeastern Minnesota and the beginning of a new life for us—and for Kay.

∽

Remembering
My Olden Days

*S*unlight shimmered on Lake Superior lying far below us as I drove onto Glenwood Street which leads into Duluth's Lakeside area and home.

"Mama, did you have cars in the olden days or did you have to ride horses?"

I looked at my three year old son next to me in the front seat of our 1953 Chevrolet. He was strapped into his car seat designed with its own small steering wheel to keep him occupied. I was in my mid-twenties and considered the olden days to be at least back in the days when my parents were children, then I thought wryly "Just like your own son is thinking."

As I turned right on Forty Fifth Avenue East beginning the descent into Lakeside, my mind drifted to Long Prairie, Minnesota in the 1930s, the setting for my "olden days."

I lived with my parents, two sisters and a brother. Life was pleasant and simple, but even in my early memories there was an ominous tone to the snatches of adult conversation I sometimes overheard.

"Hitler will be taking over Poland, just wait and see."

Then there was the talk of terrible treatment of the Jews. What could that be about? The only thing I knew about Jews was what I heard in Sunday School. I didn't understand why they were being treated badly and was afraid to ask. Too soon the rumors became reality. Poland had been invaded. England had also become involved in the fight against the Nazis on that fateful Sunday in December 1941 when our family was gathered in the living room listening to the battery operated radio. We were stunned to hear the voice of President Franklin Roosevelt telling the country about the Japanese attack on Pearl Harbor, which meant our country was entering the war.

In spite of the war, life went on almost as usual in our small town. The biggest change in our lives was the departure of a number of young men to join the armed forces, some voluntarily and some via draft called Selective Service. Weekly newspapers, newsreels, and radio were the means by which we received reports of the latest war developments.

Our world changed in 1943 when my father's Minnesota State Guard unit was called to active duty and assigned to the city of Duluth. Shortly thereafter the rest of our family followed him. When I heard of the plans to move, I hurried to tell my friend the librarian.

"What do you know about Duluth?" she asked.

Well, I didn't know much, except that it was located on Lake Superior, the largest of the Great Lakes, and much bigger than any lakes around Long Prairie. The librarian located books with pictures of the long, flat looking ore boats and the bridge that could be lifted to allow their passage into Lake Superior. She explained that the ore came from the iron range in railroad cars to the Duluth ore docks where it was loaded into the hatches of the ore boats for shipment to smelting plants in other cities. She made the city come alive in my imagination and I was excited about the move. I also knew I would miss the librarian who had been so kind to me, always taking time to answer my questions.

Grandma came to stay while Mother accompanied Daddy to Duluth to find a home and furniture for us. On her return she told us about the lake and the bridge with the piers jutting out from the harbor. We looked forward to the move.

The effect of war on the city of Duluth was dramatically different from our small town experience. We were constantly reminded that a desperate worldwide struggle was in progress. Shipments of ore from the Iron Range had intensified, steel production at the West Duluth plant was at an all-time high, and the shipyards were turning out naval and coast guard vessels in record numbers.

Although the St. Lawrence Seaway was not yet a reality, materials critical for military use were shipped in and out of Duluth. Therefore, key areas which could be potential sabotage targets, such as the Aerial Bridge, ore docks, and Thompson Dam were under constant military guard. This was the primary responsibility of my father's unit of the Minnesota State Guard.

In school, normal classroom schedules were maintained except for our few contributions to the war effort. We lined up with our money on "Savings Stamp Day" to buy stamps issued by the U.S. Government to be fastened in a folder which, when full, was turned in for a U.S. Savings Bond (commonly called War Bonds). We also brought soap, toothpaste, and other toiletries, washcloths, and small toys to fill Red Cross boxes which were shipped overseas to children in war-torn countries.

I was overjoyed to find a library in our neighborhood. The librarian didn't have as much time to devote to individual children as did my friend in Long Prairie, but oh, the books! I had never imagined such a selection and spent endless happy hours making my choices.

There were many changes in our lives outside of school. In response to simulated air raids, blackouts became a familiar routine. Blackouts were achieved by covering all windows with black curtains or shades before any lights were turned on in the house. Neighborhood air raid wardens patrolled the streets to be sure no light showed through any windows.

Basic food products and gasoline were rationed, and we learned to take those things in our stride, knowing that life was much harder for many other people throughout the world. My son's question about horses, which had prompted me to revisit these early years, didn't seem so far-fetched when I recalled that there was a man who actually drove a horse and wagon around the streets of Duluth, salvaging scrap metal and rags during the war years. Production of vehicles for other than military use had been halted for the duration of the war. Today we recycle paper, cans, and bottles (items we regard as trash) to curtail further overloading of disposal facilities. We recycled those items during the war years because of their scarcity.

We did without many luxuries that became readily available and affordable after the war, but our lives were simplified in ways that we were surprised to later learn benefitted us in the long run. The food items we now have come to believe may have an adverse effect on our health, topped the ration list and we enjoyed them sparingly because of their high cost in ration points (represented by coupons and dime-sized red and blue discs). Sugar and products made from sugar were rare, and butter was dear. Margarine was then a poor substitute, the package containing a small capsule of yellow food coloring which was to be mixed through the white substance in the hope of making it more palatable. Saccharin, the only sugar substitute available, left an unpleasant bitter aftertaste.

Adults stood in line to buy cigarettes (in short supply for civilians, the bulk of them reserved for the people in the armed forces). There was no inkling then of the toll smoking was taking on the nation's health. Many civilians purchased a gadget to "roll their own" from sacks of tobacco and cigarette papers. I sampled my first cigarettes made with a roller, tobacco, and papers pilfered by a friend from her father. Movies from the war era illustrate the influence of Hollywood on the nation's smoking habit. Cigarettes made effective props, and their use appeared glamorous to young and old alike.

Plots of city-owned land were offered to residents for use as "Victory Gardens" where produce could be grown to supplement food supplies. Fresh tomatoes, lettuce, carrots, green beans, and potatoes raised in our garden provided us with more wholesome fare than we could purchase at the grocer's. The Duluth soil and climate were not suited to growing some of our favorites, such as corn and melons, and we missed them. Mother had brought the Mason jars she used for canning when we moved, and continued to can vegetables, though not as much as in previous years. The shelves of her pantry in Long Prairie had been filled with tomatoes, carrots, green and wax beans, beets, corn, and beautiful jellies, fruits, and pickles, a treasure trove of sparkling jewels glowing in their glass jars.

We walked everywhere to save the precious gasoline ration coupons or took a bus if the distance was too far to walk. The beneficial exercise of gardening and walking was enhanced by a sense of pride that we were doing our bit for the war effort.

We proudly shopped for a service flag when my brother joined the Air Force. The field of the service flags were blue with one or more white stars (depending how many members of a family were in the armed services at the time). A silver star indicated a wounded or missing service person, and a gold star represented someone killed in action. We solemnly hung our flag in the front window. We were grateful that the star was still white when the conflict finally ended in 1945.

Our elation at the war's end was overshadowed by the terrible price exacted to achieve its closure. Germany had surrendered. Franklin Roosevelt had died in April, his end no doubt hastened by the toll the war had taken on his health. President Harry Truman authorized the use of the first atom bombs which finally led to the surrender of Japan. We were painfully aware that the unleashing of the awesome nuclear weaponry would create dramatic changes throughout the world, but the scope of those changes would be manifested in ways we could not imagine then.

Muggs

It is 1943 and I, at age nine, am being transplanted along with my parents and three siblings from Long Prairie to the city of Duluth. Viewed from the Greyhound bus window, the city sprawling along the north shore of Lake Superior seems endless. The bus descends into the heart of the city, and I'm disheartened as the buildings close in around us, blocking out the afternoon sunlight. My motion sickness, always present on long rides, is exacerbated by exhaust fumes. We have left our pet Water Spaniel behind with friends—no pets are allowed in our newly rented apartment. I know she must be missing us already and I want to go back where I belong.

~

Although I found adjustment to the confinement of city life difficult, it did offer some advantages over rural living, such as readily accessible playmates, a neighborhood library, and weekly trips to the movies. Within a year, we moved to a one-family home with a spacious yard; across the street was a large field intersected by a stream.

That was the year I was given a pet dog of my very own. A British couple, Ted York and his wife Tiny, lived next door to us. They had no children, but owned a pair of Airedale dogs. I was encouraged to visit them as often as I liked; they knew I loved the dogs, especially the male, Muggs. He was a special dog, having served in the U.S. Army Canine Corps. Brands on both ears identified him as an army dog, and he was perfectly trained. But at some point during combat training, Muggs became unable to withstand the noise of gunfire, so could not serve in the field. Usually, dogs who did not complete training had to be destroyed, but Muggs responded satisfactorily to reversal of his training and so was spared and given an honorable discharge. I was visiting the Yorks one day when Mr. York, seemingly out of the blue asked, "How would you like to have Muggs for your own?" In disbelief I looked at him and then at Tiny, whose smile lit up her round face. My heart leaped as I realized they were really offering me this marvelous dog. The generous gift had been pre-arranged with my father with the understanding that the Yorks would retain the right to use Muggs for breeding. The dogs had produced some fine puppies which had been sold, and the Yorks hoped for future litters. I couldn't think of anything more fun than having Airedale puppies next door.

Daddy made it clear that if the dog was to be mine, I would be responsible for feeding, grooming, and exercising for as long as Muggs lived. If it had been up to Mother, I'm not sure I would have been allowed to accept the dog, and Daddy did not want to hear one word about Mother being left with dog-tending chores. I made my commitment and so I had my dog. We were already best friends.

Muggs walked with me to the school corner every morning. He left me there, but was back at noon waiting for the walk home; then we repeated the ritual for the afternoon school session. Unlike my more capricious human friends and siblings, Muggs was constant in his devotion and acceptance. As long as I had Muggs, I would not be lonely.

We played Little Orphan Annie and Sandy in the big field across the street. When my playmates tired of assuming the roles of Daddy Warbucks and Punjab, I didn't much care. Since I owned "Sandy" there was no doubt who would play the starring role of Annie. If we had no supporting cast, Muggs and I would go off on our own adventures. At those times, running with Muggs in the field, it almost seemed I had returned to the open spaces of my earlier years.

I was the envy of the neighborhood kids, and more than a little proud of my special pet. Muggs was fiercely protective of me, and when a neighborhood bully began pushing me around one day, in a flash the dog had the boy flat on the ground with a paw on his chest. When the boy attempted to stand, an ominous low growl from Muggs made him reconsider. I called Muggs off and he responded immediately, returning to my side. Unhurt, the boy beat a hasty retreat. I was uneasy for a time, waiting for a possible complaint against my dog, but evidently the boy was unwilling to admit that he had been picking on a smaller kid (and a girl at that) because nothing came of the incident.

On another occasion, I discovered how far I was prepared to go to protect my best friend. Mother had sent me on an errand, and not seeing Muggs around, I went by myself. On my return, I caught sight of a man leading a dog down the alley. It was rare in those times to see a pet on a leash, which caused me to take a second look. I froze as I realized the dog was Muggs and the man was taking him away. Reacting with outrage and no thought of consequences, I sprinted down the alley after them.

As I neared the pair, I was appalled by the strange man's appearance. Despite the warmth of the summer day, he was attired in a worn-shiny dark blue suit with a battered felt hat pulled down over his brow. He was swarthy and sinister-looking, and under his cold stare I felt shivery as though a cloud had come over the sun—but no, it was still shining. The pair halted at my approach, and I glanced at the dog's ears spotting the familiar brands. There was no doubt it was Muggs, but he looked at me with no sign of recognition, and stood passively in the dust of the alley with this evil-looking man. Had he been drugged? Could this be the same dog who, such a short time ago, knocked someone to the ground in my defense? I swallowed hard, hoping my voice would not crack and betray my fear.

"Hey mister, that's my dog you've got there!"

There was no reply and no change of expression on the man's face.

"I can prove it. He's an army dog. You can see the brands on his ears."

Still no answer. My heart was pounding and Muggs continued to stand obediently, making no effort to escape. I was thrown off-balance and felt let-down by his seeming defection, but I stood my ground. Suddenly, without a word, the man bent down and removed the leash, releasing the dog. He rolled up the leash, put it in his pocket, and moved off down the alley without a backward glance. Weak-kneed, I took Muggs by the collar and led him home to his bed where he settled down and promptly went to sleep. The next morning he was alert and back to normal.

Looking back on that experience, I am still amazed the man was able to get Muggs on a leash. Had he come prepared with a leash and perhaps an appealing morsel of food laced with a sedative? Was he looking for just any dog or was Muggs his target? Could the dog's behavior represent some throwback to his military training? His eerie failure to respond to me was unbelievable and continues to haunt me.

A year later, we moved to the eastern part of the city, where I became acquainted with the owner of a small corner store. Jack was blind and his best friend was a German Shepherd guide dog named Steve. I admired Steve for his intelligence and his devotion to Jack. It was a proud day for me when Jack showed me how to approach the dog and allowed me to pet him, a privilege enjoyed by very few people.

By this time, Muggs was getting along in years. I used the leash when we walked now because of the traffic on London Road where we lived. His eyesight was failing and he stayed close to home. However, one day he ventured across the avenue and into the yard behind the corner store. This was Steve's territory to protect and, of course, the invader was attacked. No match for Steve, Muggs spent the next week in the hospital being treated for a severe throat wound. Although it healed, Muggs was weakened and I knew I wouldn't be able to keep him much longer. When Dad gently suggested it was time to let him go, I agreed; I did not want Muggs to suffer. Shortly thereafter I said my goodbyes and retreated to my room in tears before Dad took him away. It was far more painful than I could have imagined, and I swore I'd never have another dog.

I continued to visit Jack and Steve. We had that love of our dogs in common and, as far as I know, when Jack lost Steve, he never replaced him. I sometimes saw Jack walking downtown with his white cane and no dog. I did not have a dog again, but I did come to appreciate cats and enjoyed the unique personalities of several feline pets in my adult life.

It is 1998, and I am in my garden viewing with satisfaction the results of my morning's labor. Curled on the bench beside me is Sam, a black cat with emerald eyes, sharing my enjoyment of the sunshine. I have adjusted to life in the city and the fact of aging, but my thoughts wander back and in my mind's eye I see a gangling, tow-headed child racing through a field with a faithful Airedale loping at her heels—just a heartbeat behind her.

Changes of Heart

*T*hat Billy Lundgren sounds like a sick calf. Can't those boys come to the door and ask for their friends instead of bellowing like that?"

Mother never grew accustomed to kids shouting for Richard, who lived in the house next to ours, across the street from Duluth's Lincoln Park Library. The neighborhood boys each had their distinctive call as they stood in backyards summoning friends to play. Boys didn't come to my yard shouting for Donna. They would have been ridiculed by one another for seeking the company of a girl, yet they accepted me in their group whenever I showed up. A skinny tomboy, I preferred boys as playmates. I had no inkling there would soon be a change in our easy camaraderie.

Girls liked to play house with their dolls. I found this make believe boring. Whereas the athletic pursuits of the boys were real and exciting. Once in a while the girls would agree to play Monopoly, but most of them shied away from competitive games. When I talked them into going skating, they whispered and giggled around the boys and never wanted to race.

On a January day in 1945, at the sound of Billy's call "Ri-i-i-ichard!," I grabbed my skis and hurried outside. We had created a great ski slide, beginning at the steep bank on the far side of Richard's house, coming across his yard and running into a sloping vacant lot between our houses. It continued across the alley and down through an open field. Just below the alley we had built a ski jump.

Our equipment consisted of hickory skis with leather straps—no bindings and no poles. To provide some stability, we added bands cut from rubber innertubes, a scarce commodity during World War Two. We pulled the rubber bands over the toes and around the heels of our overshoes to hold our feet in the straps. Our heels still moved freely, so we were in effect down-hill skiing on cross country skis with no poles.

It was tricky to turn with our makeshift bindings, and I was proud that I negotiated the turn into the vacant lot better than any of the boys. The jump was another story. I usually hesitated too long before lifting and ended up falling over the edge. The boys had learned to time their jumps accurately and rarely fell.

Marvin and Donnie had been watching me from the bottom of the slope and Donnie called, "Jump now!"

Again, I hesitated, skied over the edge, and fell.

"You're going to ruin the ski jump," Marvin yelled as he started back up the hill.

By the time I picked myself up, they had begun arguing.

"Well she's my girlfriend," Marvin was saying, while Donnie claimed he was the favorite.

Horrified, I realized I was the object of the argument. Ignoring my protest that I was nobody's girlfriend, Marvin finally said, "Aw, you can have her, Donnie. I'm never getting married anyhow."

All the joy went out of the winter afternoon. Deflated by my instinctive awareness that nothing would be quite the same again, I shouldered my skis, announced that I would never marry anyone, and stomped to the house.

At the sink, peeling vegetables, Mother looked up in surprise.

"That was short," she commented.

I blurted out that those dumb boys were fighting over who was going to marry me. Dismayed by the concerned look that crossed her face, I was afraid she was going to talk to me about stuff I didn't want to hear. But she smiled and her voice held a note of amusement, "You're only eleven years old; I guess you have plenty of time to worry about getting married."

Mother returned to the vegetables, and I escaped to my room.

On Valentine's Day, Miss Benson placed the traditional box on a table in the front of our classroom. Decorated with white crepe paper and red hearts, it had a slot in the top to receive the valentines we would exchange with our classmates. I liked the decorations and treats, but I wasn't interested in the romantic aspect of Valentine's Day, especially this year. I barely glanced at the valentines from Billy, Richard, and Donnie. I took them home, but promptly threw them in the trash. Marvin was in a different classroom.

In the fall, I enrolled in East Junior High, where I would begin to view the opposite sex in a new light. One Friday morning at a student assembly, the auditorium stage curtains parted to reveal the "Sentimental Swingsters," the school's stage band. Strains of *Sentimental Journey* their theme song, poured from the stage, greeted by wild applause from the student fans. When I spied the handsome trombone player with dark curls and flashing smile, my heart turned over. Painfully aware that this godlike sophomore would never notice a scrawny seventh grade tomboy, I had to be content to worship him from afar.

I watched longingly as he passed in the halls with his popular friends. They were the "Big Wheels" of the school, the most popular kids, the best at sports and music. They belonged to the Delta Theta fraternity, laughing as they read the sorority publication, *Hot Copy*, between classes. *Hot Copy* reported the latest gossip and contained personality profiles featuring the Big Wheels, including Hartley, the object of my daydreams. The following year, Hartley disappeared from my world when the junior class transferred to Central High downtown.

Amazingly, he had to notice me four years later when we met on a blind date.By the time Valentine's Day of 1951 arrived, I was sold on love, marriage, and the romance of Valentine's Day. Hartley declared his love with a flowery valentine accompanied by the traditional box of chocolates; heart-shaped with a red satin cover. I opened it to discover a gold Bulova watch nestled among the candies. My fate was sealed. February 14, 2001 marked our fiftieth Valentine's Day together.

∾

Part Three:

Rising Loaves

Hart of My Heart

*T*he handsome trombone player first captured my attention when he appeared on the stage of East Junior High School auditorium during a Friday morning assembly in 1945. My interest in boys until that time had been confined to choosing them as playmates. He was a popular sophomore who did not know that I existed.

I learned his name was Hartley. He was the first person I had heard of with Hartley as a given name. His friends called him Hart. It was perfect, for he surely had touched my heart. The name seemed as warm as his smile.

The following year, Hartley moved on to Central High School in downtown Duluth, apparently leaving my sphere forever.

The usual junior high school dances brought me in contact with other boys my own age and the first awkward beginning of dating. I was tall, and junior high boys were short, not fun to dance with, but I went along with convention and played the game. I would have been more comfortable continuing to play baseball and touch football with those boys, as I had in the past.

I moved into high school with my girlfriends who spent their time angling for dates with the best looking boys.

Then one magic day, my best girlfriend, Janie, called to tell me she had been invited to a movie by Jim. She wasn't especially interested in Jim, but he had asked if I might come along on a double date with his friend, Hartley. She would have much preferred to be paired with Hartley herself, but there was no way for her to manage that. After some cajoling on my part (I think it went something like, "If you say no, I'll never speak to you again!") she agreed to accept the date.

Now I began to wonder what I was thinking of. Since seventh grade I had been holding a picture of someone I didn't really know. He was certain to be terribly conceited. With his good looks and musical talent, he no doubt was used to being the center of attention and, like many of his crowd, stuck on himself.

By Saturday night, I had convinced myself I could be in for a big letdown. When Hartley came to the door, I tried to be casual. Mother and Dad responded approvingly to Hartley's natural charm. We headed downtown in style in the Cadillac Jimmy borrowed from his dad, to the NorShor theater where midway through *Three Little Words*, Hartley casually took my hand. I felt I'd like to hold that hand the rest of my life.

In conversation later, I discovered an unassuming, lively personality, interested in ideas and people other than himself. He was seemingly unaware of his good looks, though I wonder how he could have missed the female bids for his attention. We discovered that we had both moved to Duluth from small Minnesota towns in 1943. It seemed providential. I was somewhat taken aback when he inquired what church I attended. (That was a question mothers usually asked.) As it happened, his question was well-placed, and "Lutheran" was the right answer. We had already begun an unspoken acknowledgement that we would be together always.

~

Firstborn

was surprised after the birth of our first child, Hartley, at the fierce intensity of protectiveness his arrival engendered in me. At the least provocation I consulted my Dr. Spock book, the closest substitute for an owner's manual a new mother could find in 1953. Owner's manual is the key phrase in this story. Without realizing it, I thought of this new life as our possession.

In the first weeks of his life, I guarded him jealously, fending off imagined drafts (even in midsummer) as I proudly wheeled him around the neighborhood in his carriage for his daily dose of fresh air. If he seemed to be napping longer than usual, I checked the rise and fall of the tiny chest to be certain he was still breathing. I obsessively trimmed his fingernails to avoid scratches on the delicate skin of his hands and face. I don't know how long this might have continued if it hadn't been for an incident that occurred in the month of December.

When the snow arrived toward the end of November that year, we exchanged a sled with a carved box seat for the baby carriage on our daily walks. I bundled him up in a well padded yellow snowsuit with matching cap and swaddled in a long blue scarf before surrounding him snugly with blankets.

One day well into December, when the snow was accumulating nicely to ensure a white Christmas, we went out for our morning walk. Hartley liked to go fast over the snow; it made him laugh aloud. The snow was fresh and thick and I could hear him laughing behind me. I began to walk very fast to make the ride more exciting. Suddenly he wasn't laughing anymore and the sled was suspiciously light. I stopped and turned to look at him and saw only an empty seat on the sled. In a panic I looked back down the sidewalk and saw a tiny yellow figure in a snowbank with arms and legs flailing angrily. He was howling with indignation.

That was the moment I finally got it. He did not belong to me. I was not in complete control of this person even at six months. I would have him for only a short time to nurture and guide to the best of my ability. I began to look forward to the exciting years ahead when I would watch him grow and learn to know the person he would become.

The Helicopter
Christmas

*O*ur children were blessed with several grandparents, and great-grandparents. To make identification simple for them, we encouraged the children to call the grandparents by their first names. Thus my father was Grandpa Bill.

Dad was delighted with his grandchildren and enjoyed playing with them (and their toys) as much as they enjoyed his company. As a child, I had noticed when he played with us or we were "helping" him, he had as much fun as we did and seemed like a kid himself.

Dad was a tall, slender man, dark of hair and complexion with green eyes that could on occasion, as mother phrased it, "look daggers through you." But with the children he usually displayed a mild, amused expression. His forebears were French, evidenced in Father by a nose that almost rivaled in prominence that of Charles de Gaulle. He had a manner of walking with his head poked slightly forward which made him appear to be leading with his nose in the manner of a figurehead at the prow of a ship.

As we were growing up, we children secretly (but religiously) checked our profiles in the mirror for signs that we were cursed with The Nose. We might, when angered by one or another of our siblings, suggest that their nose seemed to be getting larger. We found the prospect alarming, even though Dad seemed comfortable with his nose and found the frequent comparisons to Jimmy Durante amusing.

In 1959, the Year of the Helicopter, on Christmas morning we gathered at my sister's home for what was becoming a traditional meeting of cousins to play with the new toys. My parents were spending the holiday at our home, and so had accompanied us. Dad had already looked over my children's toys and was as anxious as the kids to see what was new at the Joneses.

The children wasted no time getting down to business. By far, the most intriguing toy that year proved to be a helicopter that was powered by centrifugal force and lifted off quite realistically when hand-cranked by a device on the helipad. Helicopters were beginning to come into their own following their use in evacuating wounded from war zones during the Korean conflict of the early 1950s. While my ten year old nephew, Tommy, proudly demonstrated his new cleverly designed toy for his younger cousin Hartley, we all watched in amazement as it lifted off its pad and hovered near the living room ceiling. Everyone was duly impressed by the performance.

No one was surprised when Grandpa Bill requested a turn at the controls. Tommy was pleased at the reaction to his chopper, and readily turned it over to his Grandfather, telling him that the directions said not to stand directly over the pad during the launch because the helicopter may rise suddenly. Heedless of the warning, Grandpa Bill began cranking vigorously with a happy smile, while Tommy stood by looking worried.

"Grandpa, I don't think you should be looking down at it," he said hesitatingly, not wanting to sound smart-alecky and risk getting the "dagger" look.

It was too late; the helicopter left the launch pad quite suddenly and rose quickly, its rotor attacking Grandpa Bill's most vulnerable facial feature. The rotation of the sharp-edged blade stopped dead when it came in contact with The Nose, but not before it inflicted considerable damage. There were numerous nicks and cuts, and profuse bleeding. Supplies were quickly assembled to clean and bind the wounds. The children were trying desperately not to giggle, and the adults were not making eye contact with one another, stifling obvious cheap shots. We knew it was painful, and thought it would be cruel to make a joke of it at Grandpa's expense, even though we knew he had a sense of humor about The Nose. When the pain had subsided somewhat, Dad was the one who finally broke the ice and gave us permission to laugh and make our tasteless observations such as, "Do you suppose there is any place open on Christmas Day that sells Band-Aids? It's going to take more than the one box we have on hand."

AND

"Wow, I sure hope it doesn't swell!"

AND

"Rudolph doesn't have anything on you, does he Grandpa?"

In spite of the pain and amidst the laughter, a great lesson was learned by the children that morning. *Do not stand over the helipad while preparing to launch!*

Hartley and the
Frigid Frogs

Chapter One

From Hay Creek to The Mighty Mississippi

artley couldn't remember a time when he didn't love being in or on the water. In 1939, he could only dream of diving and staying underwater for extended exploration. His family lived in Red Wing, Minnesota, on the Mississippi River. The river was not accessible as a regular haunt for youngsters. However, there was a municipal swimming pool and a few small bodies of water could be found within the confines of the town. Tannery Creek ran past the Red Wing Shoe Factory. Unfortunately, it carried an unhealthy sludge grayed by tannic acid waste and was off-limits to most Red Wing children. Hartley and his friends could bicycle to Hay Creek outside of town to fish (with their mother's permission).

But if you follow the Mississippi south for about thirty miles, you find big water called Lake Pepin, which is actually a widening of the Mississippi. Hartley's beloved Aunt Mae owned a fishing business in the town of Pepin, and from the time he reached school age, Hartley spent many weeks of summer vacations there. Unlike Red Wing, where access to the river was difficult, here Lake Pepin was practically right outside the door.

Pepin offered the young boy more freedom than he enjoyed at home. Crews of fishermen hired by Aunt Mae collected fish in huge seine nets for shipment by truck to markets in Chicago and New York. Hartley never tired of joining the seine crews, and his busy aunt knew the men would keep him safe without smothering him. Mae was well aware that the boy was overprotected by his mother and wanted to help broaden his horizons.

The boats left at first light when the air was still cool and the lake was a sheet of glass. The men made Hartley feel like one of the crew, but in truth as he recalls, he spent most of his time on board munching sandwiches and drinking lemonade packed by Aunt Mae in a shopping bag before he set out for the dock. When the nets were pulled in to shore, they were spread and folded in a precise manner to allow for drying, The nets were treated with tar, and during the spreading operation creosote vapors were drawn out by the sun's heat. The bare torsos of the men and the boy became burned by the sun and streaked by the vapors. Upon his inevitable return to Red Wing, Hartley would be subjected to lemon rubs administered by his mother, clucking her disapproval, in a futile attempt to erase the dirty looking streaks.

Resigned to spending the remainder of his vacation in Red Wing, he enjoyed being reunited with his playmates. His five best friends comprised his gang. That was before the word "gang" carried today's ominous implications. The gang was resourceful in creating their own recreational pursuits and their escapades, as related to me by Hartley, rivaled the antics of *The Little Rascals*, the popular film series, circa 1930. The effects of the 1929 depression still lingered and toys were scarce, so children became adept at entertaining themselves.

It was through these playmates that Hartley became intrigued with the prospect of diving. The boys were about eight years old when Robbie, displayed a suit his father had designed to use for "pretend" dives. It was cleverly fabricated from a large tin can shaped to fit around the shoulders and sported a faceplate through which to view the underwater world. A length of garden hose was secured firmly to the top of the headpiece to simulate an air hose. The bottom of the outfit was provided with loops through which a belt could be fastened to hold the contraption in place. When Hartley and the rest of the gang got a look at Robbie's diving suit, they knew the perfect place to test it would be their favorite fishing spot at Hay Creek.

It didn't take the boys long to formulate a list of the "findings" necessary to ready the suit for testing. They would need a bicycle pump and some heavy tape to fasten it to the air hose.

Muslin sugar sacks would be filled with rocks to improvise weights, and rope would be needed to tie them to the diver's ankles. They managed to assemble the necessary items, and on the first nice day, they met with their bikes and pedaled to Hay Creek, a few miles outside Red Wing. Of course, no adult had any idea of what they were up to.

Robbie, as the owner of the suit, would be the diver. Hartley was entrusted with the key assignment of manning the bicycle pump, and others would see to preparation of the weights. When all was ready, Robbie ventured into Hay Creek where water promptly began to fill the suit in spite of Hartley's frantic efforts on the air pump. When water began to rise in the glass face plate and Hartley could see only Robbie's terror-filled eyes, he gave a heroic yank on the garden hose, which mercifully held, and pulled the hapless diver to safety.

As the reader may suspect, there were parents to be reckoned with following the ill-fated venture. In spite of punishments meted out, the Hay Creek debacle was a valuable life experience. A new respect for water was added to Hartley's preparation for diving adventures yet to come.

∾

Chapter Two

From Jacques Cousteau to the Ophiems

When I married Hartley in 1951, he was enthusiastically following the exploits of a Frenchman named Jacques Cousteau. Cousteau's most fascinating endeavor was the development of an apparatus which would enable a diver to carry his own air supply underwater, allowing him to move freely, limited only by the amount of air remaining in his tank. Voila! The Aqua Lung was on the horizon. Aqua Lung was the trade name for Cousteau's invention, which was correctly described as Self Contained Underwater Breathing Apparatus. This was usually shortened to S.C.U.B.A.

By the next year, a practical model was in use and S.C.U.B.A. gear would soon be available to the public. Hartley was biding his time waiting for the day when he could get his hands on an Aqua Lung. He continued to be a stalwart admirer of Cousteau, and in years to come would follow his televised adventures as he sailed the seas of the world with his crew on their ship, the *Calypso*, exploring the ocean depths.

The birth of our first child, Hartley, in 1953 prompted us to give up apartment living, and we soon moved to a house in Duluth's Lakeside area. Hartley considered it a Gift of Providence when he discovered that one of our new neighbors was a former high school classmate who shared his interest in diving. Lee Opheim was a bachelor, which allowed him to spend his free time pursuing his varied hobbies. He lived across the street from us with his elderly parents, an only child born late in their lives. Lee shared a number of interests with his father Al, evidenced by the collection of gadgets and abandoned projects occupying every available space in basement and garage. Alma, the patient wife and mother, outnumbered by her menfolk, had only a narrow path by which to reach her basement laundry area. A huge black Labrador dog named Pal completed this interesting family.

Through Lee, Hartley discovered to his delight that two local businessmen were planning to feature the Aqua Lung in a sporting goods store they were preparing to open in Duluth's Plaza Shopping Center. Lee had already acquired equipment via mail order, but the problem remained of a source to refill the necessary compressed air tanks. At that time, Lee was shipping his tanks to Chicago for refills, an expensive and time-consuming arrangement. A tank of air was good for only about an hour of diving.

Lee had already tested the equipment in Lake Superior, with his long-suffering mother running along the shoreline, watching for bubbles. Bubbles on the water's surface assured the watcher that the diver was breathing. The cold Lake Superior waters are not friendly to divers, and protection is a necessity to survive in its depths. Suits were available for cold water diving, but Lee was a six foot, seven inch giant of a man, requiring a custom designed suit. He solved this problem by locating a source of material and pattern to make his own suit with a special adhesive to create waterproof seams. The only openings in the suit were for face and feet, with a chest opening for entry. Excess material was gathered at the chest and secured with a metal closing to keep the water out.

Within months, the new shop had opened and Hartley was outfitted with S.C.U.B.A. gear. By this time, Lee and his father had decided that they could acquire a compressor and other equipment necessary to refill air tanks and defray the cost by selling air to local divers and fire departments, who also had a need for compressed air. Soon the Opheim's dwelling on its Gladstone Street corner was a flurry of activity, especially on weekends when the divers lined up for their refills.

I frequently packed up the children (oh yes, by now we had Dawn, our second child) and went along to watch the divers. The preparations consisted of a tedious ritual. Thermal underwear went under the rubber suits, which were tight and difficult to enter. Once inside, air had to be worked out through the chest, feet, and arm openings before closing off the chest opening. Air remaining inside the suit would cause it to balloon out and prevent the diver from submerging, in spite of the lead weights worn around the waist. Masks, fins, tanks, and finally the Aqua Lungs were added.

No matter how Lee struggled to expel the air from his suit, he usually stayed on the top, arms and legs ballooned out, a black rubber giant bobbing helplessly on the waves of Lake Superior. He usually made at least one return trip to the boat to repeat the air release ritual. The sight of those early divers piqued the curiosity of visitors to the North Shore and offered a new dimension to local tourism.

With equipment available locally and Lee's compressor, there were soon enough diving enthusiasts with equipment to form their own organization through which they would offer training and begin planning exploration of Lake Superior shipwrecks, and so the "Frigid Frogs" were born.

～

Chapter Three
Watching for Bubbles

The weather was unusually warm that summer day in 1959 as I stood on the pier with my two young children. We were anxiously scanning the surface of St. Louis Bay, watching for bubbles.

"When is Daddy coming up?" my son wanted to know.

Before I could answer, a voice from the loudspeaker, attempting to maintain a light note, breezily suggested to the assembled crowd that "Hartley must have found something interesting down there to stay under so long."

We were celebrating the opening of the St. Lawrence Seaway, a marvel of modern engineering linking the Port of Duluth to ocean shipping lanes. Soon the long, flat ore boats, familiar visitors to our harbor, would be joined by ocean-going vessels from around the world.

The Frigid Frogs S.C.U.B.A. Diving Club was participating in the festivities with a presentation featuring the relatively new sport of skin diving. The organization's choice of name was obvious to anyone who had ever toe-tested the waters of Lake Superior. Charter members of the club were demonstrating the use of their Self Contained Underwater Breathing Apparatus. Jacques Cousteau's invention promised to open a whole new world of underwater exploration.

The "Frogs" were diving on the bay side of the Aerial Bridge, and Hartley was performing one of the tests that prospective members had to pass for admittance to the club. This exercise required the diver to drop his gear (mask, air tank, fins, weights, and Aqua Lung) into the water, dive in, retrieve the gear, and emerge from the water with the equipment in place. Prior to this occasion, the exercise had been practiced only in the Y.M.C.A. pool. The usual protective rubber suit used for diving in Lake Superior was not being worn for this dive, and there was no "buddy" accompanying Hartley. This was an exception to the club rule that no one went underwater without a diving buddy.

More than forty years have elapsed since then, but I can still recall the involuntary shiver that went through me, in spite of the sun's warmth on my shoulders as I peered into the dark, cold water below in search of the reassuring bubbles, evidence that an Aqua Lung was in use. With a great effort, I managed to refrain from screaming for someone to go down and investigate. Hartley's return to the surface was long overdue, and when the first bubbles finally appeared, I breathed a prayer of thanks that we still had a husband and father. However, he remained underwater, and the announcer offered a few more clever remarks. Clearly, this was not going according to plan.

Suddenly, the surface of the water was broken to great cheers from the crowd on shore and Hartley, diving gear in place, swam in. He was totally unperturbed as he deposited the heavy tank, lung, and other equipment on the pier. He flashed the familiar engaging grin as he shook his dark curls, water droplets flying in the sunlight like a handful of carelessly tossed diamonds. The children clamored for their share of attention.

"Why were you down there such a long time, Daddy? Was it real dark? Did you see any fish?"

In due course, their questions (and mine) were answered, and we heard how a display of the exercise in Lake Superior was quite different from Y.M.C.A. practice dives. When the heavy equipment hit the bay floor, the bottom water became riled making location of the equipment difficult. In addition, some of his gear had tangled on the trip down. He managed to connect the lung to the tank and take in breaths of air as necessary to stay under while he got his equipment in order. These occasional breaths did not produce enough exhaled air to make bubbles discernable on the water's surface. After he was able to don the tank and begin breathing normally, he still had his other equipment to retrieve, hence the delay in surfacing.

The diving demonstration succeeded in generating interest in S.C.U.B.A. diving, and the Frigid Frogs flourished. The story of the seaway opening demonstration was subsequently retold a number of times for the amusement of the "frog" families as we assembled weekends on the north shore of Lake Superior for diving and picnicking.

Dr. Julius Wolff, an expert on Lake Superior shipwrecks, was a helpful source of information as the group progressed to searching for sunken vessels in the big lake. The treasures retrieved usually consisted of fittings, anchors, and small pieces of hardware. The frigid waters of Lake Superior always presented a problem for the divers, but more frustrating was the limited time they could stay on the bottom. The depth of the sunken ships made it necessary to use much of the air supply to reach the wreckage. They had to reserve enough for the return trip to the surface, leaving little time for exploration and collection of artifacts.

Still, it was a great adventure we enjoyed for several years. Hartley's childhood dream had been realized, and we all had become more intimately connected to our beloved "Big Sea Water," a link which seems to be inextricably woven into the lives of all Duluthians.

∽

The Generation Gap

*M*ama, Mama, look at that funny airplane with the helicopter on the front!"

Hartley, my three year old son shouted with excitement as he watched the first propeller driven plane he had seen in his young life.

On that Sunday afternoon in 1956, most of the spectators on the observation deck at the Duluth airport were unimpressed by the lumbering passenger plane as it descended to the runway. They turned to watch the little boy's delight with amazement and amusement. Most of the observers were adults, and were still as awestruck as his parents were by the jet air traffic that had been part of our lives for a relatively short period of time.

The airport was Hartley's first choice for Sunday rides. He loved watching the jet fighter planes from the military air base adjacent to the municipal airport as the Air National Guard pilots practiced take-offs and landings. Helicopters were a familiar sight to Hartley, but not to us. Helicopters had played a part in the Korean War to rescue downed pilots and wounded servicemen during that conflict. Before that time, it had been unusual for us to sight a helicopter.

That day we began to realize how fast technology was advancing due in large part to the new developments in warfare. We were suddenly aware that we now saw few propeller driven planes landing at the airport, except for small private planes. Most of the passenger planes had been replaced with jets.

The term "Generation Gap" was not yet commonly used to describe the wide variances of generational experiences, but it is an accurate expression of our sudden awakening to the acceleration in technology that was propelling us forward with ever-increasing velocity.

〜

After the Honeymoon

*A*fter about fifteen years of marriage and beyond, I found young people wanting to know how you could stay married to one person for so long. My stock answer came to be:

"Hartley is not boring."

This remained true until the day he died.

His curiosity about the universe and everyone and everything in it kept him attuned to his environment (often distracting him from mundane activities such as lawn mowing). His range of interests amazed me: photography, skin diving, silk screening, stained glass, macramé, quilting, golfing, coin collecting, gardening, fishing, duck hunting, skiing, football, to name a few. These interests were not all pursued simultaneously, but any gear or supplies that were involved in each activity had to be kept near at hand, so they could be returned to service should the spirit move him.

This led to problems with abandoned equipment and supplies choking the storage areas of our home for fifty two years. Our attic, garage, and storage shed became legend among friends and family. When in need of an odd tool or piece of equipment, they simply called Hartley. As you might suspect, the requested item was usually hopelessly buried in the collection of momentarily abandoned interests and after a fruitless search, Hartley would have to tell the caller, "I know I have one somewhere. I just can't put my finger on it at the moment."

In addition to the equipment related to sports and hobbies, he also collected any items he came across that looked promising for use in future projects. There was a never-ending source of these treasures, as friends and neighbors found that a call to Hartley was much simpler than loading their unwanted goods and making a trip to the landfill. It had the added bonus of a small glow of good-citizen self-satisfaction as they assured themselves they were recycling.

He did agree to give up a great load of obsolete items on one occasion. Inspired by his inherent generosity, he had offered our daughter-in-law space in the basement to set up her jewelry making equipment until she could find a suitable studio in which to work. He failed to consider the condition of the space and was thus trapped into clearing it. We couldn't discard this treasure trove, but transported it to a storage shed at our place of business, which was at least one step closer to the landfill. I couldn't help wondering if his burst of generosity was prompted by Hartley's zeal to get a first-hand look at the fabrication of fine jewelry.

The question of what would be the ultimate fate of the amazing accumulation was answered on April 14, 2003 when the interior of our home was destroyed by fire. I had been reasonably tolerant with Hartley's saving habit, and now I wondered if the Hand of God had intervened by making a clean sweep which required us to begin anew.

My affinity for order and organization was as unsettling to Hartley as his exceedingly casual approach to housekeeping was to me. Yet we knew that the resulting balance kept our home and family on an even course. I managed to keep most of the clutter confined to storage areas, and Hartley kept us fascinated.

∾

A Nation Mourns

During lunch that late November, I wondered what I could possibly say to a neighbor who had lost her husband the week before in a fiery car crash. A musician returning in the early morning hours from playing a north shore supper club date, his life ended when the car in which he was riding left the curving scenic Highway 61, which was the only route by which to travel the north shore in 1963.

I was to pay his widow a visit after I sent my children back to school following lunch, and I did not feel adequately equipped to be of comfort. I seemed to lack an instinct for comforting people who were grieving. I had not lost anyone close to me, and couldn't imagine the feelings that must be assailing Jen. She was left with four children to raise. Two of them were the same ages as my children; one of those was in my Cub Scout den. My children were full of questions, and were afraid. If their friends' daddy could die, maybe they could lose their father too.

I sent the children back to school after lunch and slowly walked the block to Jen's home. The television set was on when I arrived and she didn't turn it off. It surprised me how many people failed to turn off their televisions when callers arrived (especially callers who were expected). I remembered as a child, how I was surprised in the same way by people leaving radios blaring in the background when guests arrived. It seemed these magic voices had become a part of their persona, and as such must be audible.

A soap opera was playing on the screen which was visible from the table where Jen served coffee. Perhaps it was a favorite of hers and she didn't want to miss an episode. At least it saved me from desperately casting about for the right thing to say in her devastating circumstances.

Suddenly, the program was interrupted by a news bulletin with Walter Cronkite, in a voice unlike his own, announcing that the President's vehicle had been attacked by gunfire during a parade through Dallas, Texas, as the motorcade approached Dealy Plaza. President John F. Kennedy had been rushed to Parkland Memorial Hospital, and newscaster Cronkite would stay on the air with further details as they became available. President Kennedy and his wife Jackie had flown to Dallas to campaign for Congressional Democrats. They were accompanied in their Lincoln limousine by Texas Governor John Connelly and his wife Nellie. Governor Connelly had also been hit by the gunfire.

Jen and I sat in stunned silence trying to take in what we had heard. I was concerned for her, wondering how she might be affected by another shock of this magnitude. Within minutes, Walter Cronkite, through his tears, advised the nation that President Kennedy had died of a head wound without regaining consciousness. The Governor was wounded, but stable. We finally regained our senses enough to wonder what would happen at the schools when the news was received there, and speculated that the children would probably be sent home. Certainly there would be no attempt to continue lessons for the remainder of the day. With Jen's assurance that she would be able to manage on her own, I hurried home to be there for my children.

We were right in our reasoning they would be sent home for their parents to explain as they deemed best. There seemed nothing to do but give them an honest account of events that were now playing out faster than we could comprehend each new development. In the hours and days that followed a still disbelieving audience watched the horror story unfold on television screens throughout America and the world. Lyndon Johnson was sworn in as the Thirty-Sixth President on Air Force One with his wife Ladybird and Mrs. Kennedy at his side. The dead president was taken aboard to be transported to Walter Reed Hospital in Washington, D.C. The flight left immediately following the swearing-in.

A shooter was apprehended and identified shortly after the attack. Lee Harvey Oswald was accused of attacking the motorcade with a high-powered rifle from the window of a book depository. Evidence, including the rifle were recovered and Oswald was arrested and jailed. A Dallas police officer was killed during the chase to apprehend the suspect. The following day as Lee Oswald was being transferred to another facility, we watched as a man stepped forward from a group of spectators and shot at point-blank range, killing Oswald on the spot. The killer was immediately taken into custody, and was soon identified as Jack Ruby, a local nightclub owner.

∾

An interesting side-note here was that this real-life murder, carried on prime time television news, gave rise to the delusion that we could stop being concerned about the negative effects of violence in television entertainment. The reasoning? Now that we knew the difference between make-believe violence and the real thing, our children would not be harmed by exposure to "pretend" violence.

∾

We saw the sad procession of mourners who waited through the night to file by the casket of President Kennedy in the rotunda of the Capitol. There was the funeral with the mourners walking behind the horse-drawn caisson through the Washington streets.

A commission appointed to investigate the assassination was headed by Chief Justice Warren and designed to provide closure to the rampant speculation and theories being put forth. The Warren Commission did not achieve its purpose, and I see little hope that we will ever hear the real story behind this national tragedy. There have been television productions, movies, and books too numerous to imagine spelling out various plots and speculations about who was responsible for the murder of John F. Kennedy.

The only fact on which every person I have heard comment on the tragedy agrees, is that each of us knows exactly where we were and what we were doing at the time of the assassination; a moment frozen in time.

∾

Searching
For Gwendolyn

*L*ate on a July evening in 1996, I was surprised by a phone call from my brother, Jerry. It was unusual for him to call that late. He sounded excited as he told me he had just received a call from a woman in Minneapolis, who had been enlisted by her adopted brother, Joel, to help him in his search for his birth mother. She had found Jerry's name in the Duluth phone directory and asked him if he had a relative named Gwendolyn. Joel lived in Michigan but knew Gwendolyn's family had come from Minnesota. His hope that his sister might find the family through Minnesota telephone directories was realized when, after a few questions, Jerry knew without a doubt that Joel was looking for our cousin, Gwendolyn.

In 1996, Joel was thirty-four, but his quest began some years earlier. As children, he and his sister had been told by their parents that they were adopted. They had raised their children well, yet Joel's curiosity about his birth mother prompted him to poke around in the study until he found his birth certificate in the desk. Gwendolyn's name jumped off the page, and he knew he must try to find her. The "unknown" designation of his birth father did not surprise him, but at least he had a chance to locate his mother, as her maiden name was clearly stated on the document. When he proposed the idea of initiating a search for her, he was surprised by the vehement reaction of his parents. They seemed to feel threatened by the prospect of finding Gwendolyn.

Joel was disappointed, but he kept his peace. He could not abandon his plan to search for Gwendolyn, even though he felt enormously disloyal to his adoptive parents. He confided this to his sister, who understood and agreed to help him. His first tentative efforts to locate his mother were obscured by the overwhelming guilt that accompanied his quest, but he bided his time. He did not begin his systematic search until he had a family of his own.

I don't know how long he had pored over Michigan and Wisconsin phone books, while his sister worked on Minnesota from her home in Minneapolis. It seemed he could have pursued more direct and less tedious routes to achieve his purpose, but I suspect he was experiencing a certain ambivalence in embarking on those final steps, which once taken could not be retraced. When Jerry had verified that Gwendolyn was the youngest child of Dad's brother, our Uncle Glenn, Joel's sister was elated and gave him the phone number to call in Michigan to make contact with Joel. Jerry, of course, was stunned, but recovered sufficiently to call Joel and invite him to bring his family to the summer cabin Jerry owns near Duluth. They would spend the week, and our family would drive out on the weekend to meet them.

How could I have thought I knew everything about everyone in my family? Even with all the publicity in recent years concerning the changes in regulation of information surrounding adoptions, it had never crossed my mind that we would find ourselves waiting to meet a family member totally lost to us since birth. This was not the sort of thing that happens in your own family. Then I had to laugh at myself. Why not in your own family? After the shock abated, I began to think of what we could do to help fill in the blanks of this young man's background.

It didn't take long for my initial excitement to fade, as I recalled the history of Gwendolyn and her family. The first fact that jolted me back to reality was that some twenty years ago, Mother had called me from Minneapolis, where she and Dad lived, to say they had heard from Gwen after many years of silence. She kept in touch with them for some time, but never divulged the fact she had given birth to a son. Then one of Mother's letters informed me that Gwen was terminally ill, and shortly thereafter she wrote that Gwen had died. Now I was appalled that my recollection of the facts was insufficient to tell Joel with any assurance whether his mother was living or dead.

The story of Gwen and her sister Connie, suppressed so long, came rushing to my mind. Transported back a half-century, I was bent over my embroidery with my paternal grandmother at my side. She was updating Mother on the latest transgressions of her other daughter-in-law (Connie and Gwen's mother). I always got an earful of gossip, much of which I could not understand, when Grandma came for her annual summer visit. She schooled us in a variety of needlework skills, all the while regaling Mother with endless accounts of the character flaws exhibited by other family members. Mother went about her work, never breaking concentration on the task at hand, saying things like, "Hummmm…. Is that so?" or "Oh, My!"

We loved Grandma and she was patient with us, guiding our unskilled fingers wielding embroidery needles or crochet hooks though overworked yarns and fabric. Yet, I was sure that when Grandma's round of visits brought her back to Benson where most of the relatives lived, *Our* family would be the target of Grandma's sharp tongue.

Uncle Glenn, Connie and Gwen's father, was the youngest of Grandma's children. Though generally foregoing any outward displays of affection, Grandma doted on Uncle Glenn, who was handsome and charming. Perhaps Grandma's conviction that he could do no wrong contributed to the self-indulgence that eclipsed his physical appeal and mental agility. His dependence on alcohol finally alienated him from his family, and ultimately caused his early demise, but not before his wife was stricken with cancer and preceded him to the grave, leaving her two young daughters.

Their father was not fit to care for the girls, and the family members in Benson were unwilling to assume responsibility, so my parents were called. It did not enter my mind that we would not take them in, but in fact we didn't. At age twelve, I could not imagine myself and my sisters in our cousins' place. How could our parents be so heartless? I knew that Dad had left the final decision to Mother, who would bear the daily responsibility of their care, and I secretly felt she had made a cruel choice. I could not reconcile her decision with the teachings of the Christian church we attended weekly at her insistence. When I learned our cousins had gone to foster homes, I tried not to conjure up pictures of them being separated and living with strangers as they mourned the loss of their mother.

Was I going to tell all this to Joel? Of course not. Our first step in preparing for his visit was to sketch a chart of our paternal family. All of my father's generation was gone, but photos remained and many cousins still lived in

Minnesota. We scoured family albums looking for photos to correspond to our chart. I hoped that Joel's expectations would not exceed the reality of meeting people who were virtually strangers to him. After all, he had a complete family back in Michigan, the only family he had ever known.

My husband was an interested spectator to this unfolding drama. It was an experience neither of us expected to encounter, and he added his suggestions as the week wore on. He agreed it would serve no purpose to focus on the negative aspects of Gwen's childhood, but we would offer Joel the facts that would be helpful to himself and his family.

Saturday morning finally arrived and we headed for the lake. As we neared the cabin we saw Joel's two little girls playing with the younger children from our family. (I wondered if they knew.) We entered the kitchen and I looked into familiar eyes that searched my face for any sign of resemblance to him. There was no mistaking the eyes of Dad's family as we looked at Joel.

He was eager to see the photos we could offer. There was no awkwardness or uneasiness in our communication, but Joel did acknowledge that his feelings of disloyalty to his parents remained. He had not told them the real purpose of this trip, and had not yet decided whether he would ever tell them. Although puzzled, we didn't question him about their attitude regarding his wish to find Gwen. We could only offer our understanding if he wished to forego any further contact.

I noticed Joel's wife played with the children outside the cabin during much of our visit, and I wondered if this was to avoid arousing their curiosity about our identity. Future visits would no doubt require explanations that would put the children in an unfair position if the truth was to be kept from their grandparents.

Joel did have an opportunity to glean some information about his birth mother's background, along with the unfortunate facts of his grandfather's addiction. We felt this could be important for him to know even though it revealed some painful facts of his mother's early life.

He did not keep any of the pictures we brought lest his parents might somehow see them and feel betrayed. Our visit ended on an almost wistful note. When I asked Joel if he was happy he had made the search, he wasn't sure. He knew we could not recapture the lost years, and yet he was obviously glad to have found us. I knew the cloud of his guilt still cast a shadow over his visit. It seemed sad to me that he should be burdened with feelings of disloyalty, in addition to coping with the other strong emotions evoked by this meeting.

In 1999 our cousin Sandy began work on a genealogy of Dad's family, and has located the grave of Joel's mother. Sandy has been able to supply much more information than we had to offer him. Easier access to the Internet has expedited transmission of information to keep Joel updated. He has kept in touch with us and advised us that his adoptive father has died. He knows he is welcome to visit us again any time. Perhaps one day he will.

Farewell
to Fantasy

We were chilled by the unseasonably cold wind as it attacked through unseen chinks in the window casings causing the drapes to billow with each gust. Our four-day vigil at Mt. Sinai Hospital in Minneapolis was nearing its end.

Mother was undergoing emergency open heart surgery in the waning hours of that March night in 1981. She was eighty one years old, and chances of her survival were slim. We knew she did not wish to live as an invalid. Yet, we kept hoping for a miracle. When the weary surgeon appeared sometime after 2 A.M., his slumped shoulders and downcast eyes told us Mother was gone even before he uttered a word.

My youngest sister Vonnie, from Rochester, New York, my older sister Wanda, and I, both from Duluth, returned to our suite at the Curtiss Hotel. We had settled Dad with our brother Jerry in Mother and Dad's home nearby for what was left of the night. Exhausted, we fell into our beds until a sniffle from my sister brought us running to her king-sized bed where we clung together sobbing softly before finally falling into fitful sleep. Of course, we wept not for the mother we had lost, but for ourselves.

The next two days passed in a blur of ritual calls to family and struggling to make arrangements. We were familiar with Minneapolis, but arranging for funeral services, reception, and flowers was beyond our experience in this city. Our knowledge of Minneapolis was limited to shopping centers, hotels, and restaurants. We left our brother to keep Dad company in the living room while we approached Mother's closet to deal with the sad task of selecting a dress for her burial. Wanda was looking in

Mother's jewelry drawer for a pin to complement the chosen dress when she suddenly called, "Look! The brownie pin. Remember? We couldn't believe our eyes the day we found the brownies." Wanda and I had been shopping a few years earlier when she spotted them. Now we were cheered by the sight of the brownie smiling as he slept in a curled autumn leaf fashioned into a pin.

~

The years fell away and we were transported back to the autumn days of our early childhood when the leaves were falling and Mother sang to us:

"Come little leaves, said the wind one day, Come o'er the meadows with me and play.

Put on your dresses of red and gold.

Summer is gone and the days grow cold."

She told us if we were very quick to open the curled leaves that had fallen, we would find tiny brownies hiding inside. Half-believing her, we chased the leaves and tried to unfold them quickly enough to catch one, to no avail. It was thirty-five years later in a Duluth Hallmark store, when we finally captured them.

We decided to buy one for each of us and one for Mother. I expressed some doubt that Mother would understand.

"She might think we are acting a little peculiar and even wonder if we're experiencing early *Change*," I suggested to Wanda.

Mother referred to menopause as *The Change* to which she attributed any unusual feminine actions or reactions. But Wanda planned to bring the pin on her next trip to Minneapolis, certain Mother would be delighted by our discovery of the brownies. On her return, Wanda reported that Mother looked at her in surprise when presented with the pin and declared she only sent us on the brownie hunt to keep us occupied saying, "You'll think of anything you can to amuse three active children when you're busy."

In my next phone conversation with Mother, she asked me about Wanda.

"Do you think she could be starting *The Change* early? I know she's young, but she brought me an odd pin—a brownie in a leaf—and talked about how I sent you kids out brownie hunting."

I reassured Mother by telling her that I was with Wanda when she spied the brownies and we thought it would be fun to buy them as mementos of the great stories Mother had entertained us with when we were little.

～

Finding the brownie among Mother's jewelry made that bleak March day more bearable. It was a relief to share our first laugh in days. Wanda selected a sliver brooch, pinned it to the collar of Mother's turquoise dress, and closed the jewelry drawer.

Planning the funeral service held little comfort for us. It was as cold as the pastor of the ultra-strict Norwegian Lutheran church Mother attended, but we were warmed by the love expressed by family and friends.

We steeled ourselves for the inevitable evening visitation. Wanda took our hands and, at her urging, the three of us approached the coffin. I managed to stand there quietly with my sisters, knowing Mother was not really there. I noted with satisfaction that the dress did look lovely. Then to my horror and disbelief, Wanda slowly reached into the casket. She lifted the collar of Mother's dress, turned to us and smiled. So did we when we saw what the collar had concealed. The brownie reposed there in his curled-up leaf sleeping peacefully on Mother's shoulder.

～

No Good Deed Goes Unpunished

$\mathcal{M}$y mother-in-law, Grace, had a fondness for small animals that I was sure exceeded her love of people. The soothing tones of her voice coaxed birds and chipmunks to come to her and eat from her hand.

For most of her life, household pets had been some of Grace's best friends, but a patriarchal post-retirement pronouncement by her husband, Bernard, placed their home off limits to animals of any kind. He was compulsively tidy, constantly fussing over pressing his suits and shining his shoes. Since his retirement, he had taken to patrolling the house for lapses in housekeeping, clucking over an errant dust mote here and chasing down a few counter crumbs there.

In the fall of 1979, after a few petless years during which Grace tried to wheedle Bernard into relenting, she spotted a pair of finches in a pet store window and managed to lure Bernard inside. Once in the store, in spite of a musty odor around the finch cages that caused him to wrinkle his nose in distaste, he was unable to withstand her pleas. They left the store loaded down with a pair of finches in a covered cage and an ample supply of seed, cuttlebone, gravel, assorted finch toys, and the mandatory finch owner's manual. Bernard had the foresight to include pre-cut papers for the cage floor, to eliminate the need for cutting up discarded newspapers.

In short order, Grace became well-versed in the care of finches. She studied every piece of literature she could locate on their nature and habits. She learned that bits of lint and thread placed in the cage would stimulate their nesting instinct, thereby encouraging mating and egg production. Bernard was still smiling at Grace's delight in the birds, but the messiness of the cage offended him with its spilled seed and water and bird droppings spread over its paper-carpeted floor. The prospect of hatching finch eggs did not appeal to him, but that didn't deter Grace.

One day I stopped for a visit to discover that the finches were busy building a nest. A short time later an egg appeared that was perhaps the size of a child's fingernail. I heartily congratulated Grace for her cleverness in promoting this little family. Personally, I wasn't impressed with the finches. They were rather dull looking, didn't sing, and had little personality. Now that they were finally doing something, I observed the finches with more interest. Grace was busy studying the characteristics of finch parenting. She was alarmed to learn that male finches had an unpleasant tendency to kill their offspring. The manual strongly recommended early separation of the young bird from its parents, but Bernard would not hear of a second cage. It seemed, if the egg hatched, the new finch would have to take its chances with a potentially cannibalistic father.

Amazingly, the egg opened to reveal an incredibly tiny, ugly bird. Its exceedingly disastrous appearance led me to understand why a father bird might be prompted to take it out of existence. However, my maternal instinct prevailed. I had a bird cage in the attic which had housed my son's parakeet in earlier years, so I offered to take over the care and feeding of the creature when it was mature enough to leave the nest.

When Grace pronounced the bird ready to travel, we brought the cage and placed the bird inside. Then with the cage swathed in blankets against the November chill, we made the trip to Gladstone St. He (we were still guessing at the gender) appeared to weather the trip well. We were generously supplied with the necessities for his survival. Grace had shopped for everything a baby finch could wish for.

I faithfully gave him fresh water and food every morning, cleaned his cage, and supplied him with gravel and cuttlebone. His cage was covered every night to prevent drafts from reaching the sleeping bird. He looked well, but I thought he must be lonely.

In spite of my best efforts, one morning I removed the cover to find him a sad little heap on the bottom of his cage. My husband, Hartley, could not imagine what had gone wrong, but was convinced I had somehow failed as a surrogate finch mom. "Are you sure he had food?"

"Yes."

"How about water?"

"Of course."

"Did he have cuttlebone? Maybe you forgot the cuttlebone."

"No, I didn't forget. He had cuttlebone."

"How about gravel. You know they have to have gravel."

"He had gravel."

"Did you cover the cage every night?"

"Yes, I covered the cage."

"What are we going to tell Mother?"

"How about the truth? The bird died," I countered.

"I know! This will be our story—"

"Wait," I interrupted him. "We don't need a story. The bird died. Period."

"Well, she'll think you did something wrong for it to die like that."

"Never mind. My conscience is clear. Next time we see her I'll simply tell her and offer our sympathy."

A few days passed with Hartley intermittently interrogating me about the bird.

"Are you sure he had gravel? You didn't forget to feed him, did you? Are you sure he was covered every night?" and on and on.

Meanwhile, our son Hartley Jr., who was visiting from Georgia for a few weeks over the holidays, held his peace as he listened to the tirade of questions. Finally he could stand it no longer. In his twenty six years, he had not used vulgar or offensive language in front of his mother, but now with a look of disdain, he confronted his father with:

Dad, is it really worth giving her the third degree over a fucking finch?

෴

Part Four:

Breaking Bread

Portage to Bluet

*W*e sat around the oilcloth-covered table in the kitchen of the main lodge at Gull Wing Lake on a midsummer evening in 1959. The lodge in Ontario, Canada was owned by friends, Joan and Bill Smith. My husband Hartley and I, along with mutual friends Mary Ann and Ron Weber, were spending the week visiting and fishing. Ron was a sales representative for Pflueger Fishing Products. He was an expert fisherman, and anyone fishing with Ron was sure to come home with a limit of fish. He had been trying out a new bait he discovered at Gull Wing called the Rapala, which would in years to come make him wealthy. But that is another story. This evening we were planning a trip to a remote lake called Bluet to fish for walleyes. Gull Wing was the lake to fish for lake trout.

"Who's going to Bluet tomorrow?" Bill queried.

Hartley and the Webers said yes.

I agreed, "If the weather is nice."

This qualification was met with a withering reply, "The plans are made the night before and there is no backing out!"

I quickly stated my intention to go on the portage to Bluet, come hell or high water.

Morning dawned chilly and gray with a brisk breeze and a threat of rain. It felt mighty cozy having breakfast in the main lodge with the fragrance of wood burning in the big iron cookstove warming the lodge while bacon sizzled on top. I would have enjoyed lingering over coffee, but we wasted no time getting started. We had two portages ahead of us with a canoe trip down Needle Lake between portages. Bill kept two canoes on Needle and two boats with motors on Bluet for the use of his guests. These lakes were not accessible by road, so the surrounding lands were not inhabited by people—only wildlife.

We distributed the gear between the four of us for the hike through the woods. The heavy air was perfumed by the scent of pine needles as our footfalls were nearly soundless on the thick carpet of decayed leaves and pine needles beneath us.

Needle Lake is as narrow as its name and shallow. As we approached, a great blue heron lifted off from the swampy surrounds, startled by our sudden appearance in his domain. We stowed our lunch and equipment in the canoes and silently paddled the length of Needle. Our next portage to Bluet was shorter and it was about 9 A.M. when the lake came into view. As we suspected, the water looked choppy. We had already decided that Mary Ann and I would stay on shore if the lake looked at all rough, as Mary Ann was just three months into her first pregnancy. We had brought reading material and were prepared for a day of visiting and relaxing with our books.

Ron and Hartley set out to fish after propping the second boat up against trees to create a shelter for us in case of rain. They would fish until noon, and then come in to have lunch with us. We were happy visiting until the men returned for lunch, and encouraged them to go out again in the afternoon as they had not caught their limit yet.

We were well-protected under the boat from the intermittent sputtering rain showers and were reading our books when suddenly Mary Ann exclaimed, "What was that?"

"I didn't hear anything."

"Someone coughed," she said firmly.

"It couldn't possibly be someone coughing. We are the only people on the lake," I said, trying to reassure her.

"There it is again," Mary Ann insisted.

"Maybe we should stop reading, and visit for awhile," I suggested.

I was becoming a little spooked, but neither of us considered emerging from under the boat to investigate. We continued to catch up on our visiting. Mary Ann and Ron had moved to Minneapolis, and we didn't see them often so we had a lot to talk about. Hartley and Ron returned at about 3 P.M.

(the witching hour, as that was the time we needed to start back to reach the lodge in time for dinner). They displayed their catch with the pride of good fishermen, and asked if we had stayed dry and comfortable.

"We were fine, but Mary Ann kept hearing sounds like coughing," I told them. A peculiar look passed between Hartley and Ron, and they walked around to the back of the boat inspecting the ground.

"You had a visitor all right," Ron said. "It's a good thing you stayed under the boat."

There in the rain-softened earth were fresh hoof prints. Our cougher was a moose, and by the size of the prints, a *large* moose. But, by the time we reached the lodge to tell our story at dinner, the moose had become even larger.

∾

A Day on
the Mountain

On an April morning in 1978, I awake to the sound of distant muffled explosions. Charges are being set off on areas of the the mountain where unstable snow conditions create avalanche hazards. Setting off the avalanche in a controlled situation lessens the danger to skiers. I find the sound reassuring. I leave my warm bed where Hartley sleeps on, and look out the window which frames the imposing Mount Daly, austere and unapproachable under its pristine snow-frosted surface.

I listen for sounds of stirring in the house on Faraway Road. Of course there are none. I am usually the first one up eager to get to the ski area. It's too early to shower with everyone trying to sleep, but I know there is one household member who will be glad to see me. I pull on a sweat suit and creep upstairs to the kitchen to brew coffee. Sure enough, there is Puss, the family cat, sitting at the dining room window gazing at the small balcony where a sleek blue Stellar's jay is breakfasting on seeds provided for their feathered friends by our hosts, Joan and Bill Smith. I prepare coffee, laughing as I watch Puss who makes funny clicking sounds with his teeth in hopeful anticipation of catching a fat jay. He joins me by the window to savor the view of the vast Snowmass Mountain all around us. The house clings to the mountainside ten miles from Aspen, Colorado and just a few switchbacks from the nearest chairlift. I feel very close to heaven.

Soon the others begin to appear in the kitchen, and the morning ritual begins. We prepare our breakfast of fruit, hot cereal, toast, and coffee while listening to the radio weather report and rundown of snow conditions at various ski areas in the vicinity of Aspen. We talk over plans for the day, and Joan reminds us that she has made reservations for dinner at the Pepper Mill in Snowmass Village one of our favorite dining places. She made the reservation weeks earlier, the only way to be assured of an opening at this fabulous spot.

The kitchen is tidied up and it's time to collect our gear, taking care to forget nothing for our long day on the mountain. I go over my mental checklist; lip balm, tissues, money, and a baggie of trail mix. Finally, with these necessities stowed away in the intricate pockets built into ski clothing, we don the stiff ski boots, hats and mitts, and sunglasses. The skis and poles are secured in the car-top carrier and we are off to the Elk Camp parking lot and chairlift.

"Let's take one run down Sandy Park and then head over to High Alpine so we can have lunch at Gwyn's," Joan suggests.

The chairlift system is designed to enable skiers to travel from one area to another (if you know where the lifts connect). It is imperative that you get back to the area where you left your car by the time the lifts shut down, or you might find yourself stranded on Naked Lady at High Alpine when you should be taking Grey Wolf to the bottom of Elk Camp! I pick up a trail map at the ticket booth in case I should become separated from the others.

We will send Bill off alone to ski the yellow diamond runs he favors. They are classified "beyond difficult." Bill is a confident, strong expert skier, and we don't expect him to spend the entire day skiing at our level. We encourage Joan to accompany him, which she will do for part of the day, then we'll meet at Gwyn's High Alpine restaurant for lunch. Hartley and I are more comfortable skiing the blue (more difficult) with a black (expert) here and there.

Joan and I ride together on the lift so we can visit during the half hour trip up the mountain. The sun is hot as we near the top and we unzip our jackets for the remainder of the ride.

"Could anything be more wonderful than spring skiing in the Rockies?" I think to myself.

My enthusiasm may be in part due to a certain euphoria produced by the altitude (the "Rocky Mountain High" John Denver sang about), but I can't imagine a more beautiful place in all the world than the Rockies in springtime.

At the top of the mountain we gather to drink in the panorama before us prior to beginning our descent down Sandy Park. My bindings respond with a satisfying click, as I slide my boots in place. As we cruise along the familiar trail, my skis feel wonderful carrying me through turns in the perfect snow. We all feel the same exuberance, and barely pause to rest throughout the run. When we finally stop, Bill points a ski pole in the direction of the cutoff to the High Alpine lift and we leave Elk Camp. Hartley and I ride the lift together now with agreement to meet the Smiths at 11:30 for lunch.

"Whoever gets there first, try to get a table outside on the deck," Bill calls in parting.

We have time for two trips down and back up High Alpine before lunch. We take our time now, stopping to admire the places we love on the mountain as we make our way down. We decide on an expert run for our second trip down. Following this arduous descent, we are ready to look for a spot on the deck to have lunch. We find an empty table and watch the Whiskey Jacks beg for scraps from the diners around us while we wait for Bill and Joan. They arrive shortly, and the men go in to buy our lunch selections while Joan and I stay outdoors and hold the table. At 11:30 skiers begin to desert the slopes and flock to the restaurants along with the Whiskey Jacks and Magpies. On beautiful days, the outdoor tables are at a premium. We take off our jackets and bask in the spring sunshine. We have a light lunch in anticipation of an afternoon of skiing and the gourmet Pepper Mill dinner this evening.

After lunch, we take one last run down High Alpine before moving back to Elk Camp to finish our day of skiing. Only a short way down the run, a young boy passes our group skiing too fast with the confidence and exuberance of youth. In his attempt to regain control, he suddenly cuts in front of Hartley who is leading us. Hartley sets his ski edges for a quick stop, but a collision is unavoidable. The boy falls and goes skidding down the mountain. When he comes to a stop, we ski down to him, reaching him just as his mother, who was behind him on the run, approaches. She witnessed the incident from her vantage point higher on the mountain. The boy, who appears to be nine or ten years old, is whimpering and we are fearful he is hurt. We move back as his mother talks to him and gets him on his feet. Shortly, she comes over to address Hartley.

"I'm sorry he cut you off like that. He is suffering from embarrassment rather than pain. His father is a doctor and will check him over when we get back to the condo. This wasn't your fault; please go ahead and enjoy the rest of your day."

We finish our run, greatly relieved that we didn't have to use one of the telephones stationed in various locations on the mountain for the purpose of reporting injuries to the ski patrol.

It is nearing 3:30 and we debate about catching the last chairlift to the top for one final run.

"No," Joan says, "We're getting tired, and that's how injuries occur—by pushing to get in one more run. Remember we still have to ski to the bottom of the mountain."

We reluctantly agree that it is a good time to quit for today. Back at the house, it feels wonderful to pull off the confining ski boots and head for the shower. A bit of cheese and crackers and Coors beer are a welcome treat to tide us over until dinnertime.

A few hours later at the Pepper Mill, we sit in the comfortable chairs in the lounge where our host entertains his guests at the piano. Bob seems to particularly enjoy this aspect of restaurant ownership. We move to the dining room to enjoy the elegant courses of appetizer, soup, salad, entree, and dessert, presented in civilized portions. A fine wine selection accompanies the meal. We ask our waiter if the chef might divulge the contents of the salad dressing. He goes off to the kitchen and soon returns with an invitation to join the chef in his kitchen to watch him prepare the dressing. We eagerly accept his gracious offer and are given the recipe as we watch him whisk his special dressing.

On the drive back to Faraway Road, we agree that this has been one of our most magical days on the mountain. We look forward to tomorrow when we will spend the day visiting Aspen for lunch and shopping at our favorite haunts.

Before I climb into bed, I take a last look out the window where Mount Daly stands guard, shadowy now in the pale moonlight with the village lights twinkling far below.

The Fire Run

This story was related to my son, Hartley, by my father-in-law, Bernard Schilling, who was born in 1906 in Red Wing, Minnesota, and lived there for the first forty years of his life. The story takes place in 1914 when Bernard was a boy of eight. When Hartley finished recounting this adventure, he quoted his grandfather as saying, "I don't recall what I did last week, but I remember this as if it happened only yesterday."

≈

At the time of Bernard's birth to Charles and Freda Schilling in 1906, their hometown of Red Wing, Minnesota, on the Mississippi River offered children an intriguing environment in which to explore and learn. Red Wing was an exceptionally beautiful town with bluffs, ponds, streams, and caves for youngsters to investigate during the summer months. Winter excitement was provided by bobsled rides down the long Malthouse Hill. The means of transportation was still primarily horse and buggy or horse-drawn wagon.

Bernard, an only child, was called Ben by his friends, but his straight-laced mother would call him only by his given name all of her life. By the time he reached school age, Ben had a best friend, Arty, whose father was the fire chief in Red Wing, and the boys loved to visit him at the fire hall. The Red Wing firefighting equipment consisted of a horse drawn wagon carrying hand pumpers and ladders. A well-polished bell warned street traffic and pedestrians to make way for the firewagon.

The space housing the equipment was permeated by a pleasant leathery smell emanating from harnesses waiting in place on the ceiling. When the fire alarm sounded, the harnesses were immediately lowered as the horses were led from stables adjacent to the fire hall to their places in front of the wagon. These positions were precisely marked on the floor to insure exact placement of the harnesses. The back of the wagon was covered by a heavy tarp when not in use. As fire chief, Arty's father did not ride on the wagon, but attended fires in his own special buggy.

By the time the boys were eight years old, their awe at the sight of all this paraphernalia began to diminish. So, on one of their visits to the fire hall, emboldened by the fact that no one was in the vicinity of the firewagon, they climbed aboard. Absorbed in their fantasy world of firefighting, imagine their fright when they heard the fire alarm sound. Peering out from under the tarp, they saw the horses led in and the harnesses coming down from the dimly lit ceiling to be snapped into place. They heard voices and footsteps of firemen preparing to board the wagon. Staving off their inevitable discovery, the boys just in time managed to hunker down between the equipment as the firemen jumped aboard.

It was a noisy and terrifying ride to the fire location. Racing down Main Street with the bell clanging furiously, the boys were jostled and bumped as the wagon careened around corners to the sounds of horses' hooves and wagon wheels accompanied by rattling equipment. As they lurched to a halt, Ben and Arty realized the moment was at hand when their presence would be revealed. The tarp came off and they stood up blinking sheepishly as the fire chief dismounted from his buggy, wide-eyed at the sight of the stowaways. They were whisked off to a seat in his buggy where they had ample time to contemplate their foolhardy behavior amidst shouted orders and the sounds of the pumping equipment as firemen fought the crackling flames. How the boys wished they were viewing the excitement from across the street with the other spectators who had followed the firewagon to the scene.

The trip home was not quite what an eight-year-old boy might have anticipated a ride in the fire chief's buggy would be.

Joan Judeen in Her
Flying Machine

In 1944 at age ten when I learned of a proposed expedition to search for Noah's ark, I wanted to be among those present for the discovery. When my ardor for that project cooled, I was sure the ten dollars Father shelled out for my deluxe *Chemcraft* chemistry set would not be wasted. I began to see myself as the next Madame Curie, making a scientific discovery of epic proportions. Never mind that I found science the least appealing subject in my fifth grade curriculum. These childhood fancies, which I now recall with amusement, faded in due time. But there are certain enviable people like my friend, Joan Judeen Smith, who early in life develop a passion for a goal, the achievement of which is never in doubt.

Our friendship began in the 1950s when we were in our early twenties, newly married to young men whose friendship had begun in junior high school. The four of us were comfortable together, and it didn't take long for Joan to confide in me a dream, held close from childhood, to pilot small planes. She read everything she could find on the life of her idol, Amelia Earhart, and was determined that some day she would learn to fly.

I was impressed. I had trouble finding my way around well-marked city streets. Contemplating the prospect of ascending alone into the space above earth and finding my way back made me queasy. She stated her intention quietly, but confidently. I could easily picture Joan accomplishing anything she set out to do. I had observed her capacity to apply total concentration to whatever she set out to learn and absorb and retain it with amazing alacrity. This quality afforded her the ability to focus quickly on a problem, analyze it, and resolve it decisively and efficiently. I was convinced she would make an excellent pilot.

By 1960, we each had two children and were deeply involved with business, careers, and homes. Though we shared many interests, we also took part in a number of independent activities. We might take a trip together, then not see each other for weeks. When we met again, there never seemed to be enough time to catch up on our talk of reading, current projects, or ideas. But the dream was not forgotten. She kept a picture of Amelia Earhart on her piano and Joan's husband, Bill who had piloted his own plane for many years was a source of encouragement.

Our children were grown when she announced that she had arranged to start flying lessons. I enjoyed a thrill of vicarious pleasure at the thought of her up there in her small plane. Of course there were the naysayers among our acquaintances who were sure she'd break her neck. They were the objects of our good-humored pity.

She took lessons, pored over textbooks, passed the written tests, and was soon qualified to fly solo. I had no desire to pilot a plane myself, but that did not diminish the pride I felt for my friend's accomplishment. Now she was going to the next level, working for the rating that would allow her to carry passengers. When she proclaimed herself ready for this next step, she expressed one concern:

"I have to find someone willing to take the initial flight."

Without hesitating, I volunteered to be her first passenger.

"Do you mean you would trust me with your life?"

It was obvious that she considered this a serious business, which was enough to reassure me that I would be in good hands. We agreed that she would call me on the first day of good flying weather and I would slip away from the office to fly with her.

One spring afternoon as I sat working at my desk, the call came. "Can you get away?"

I left word at the front desk that I'd be out for a while and hurried out to the street where Joan waited.

Although we didn't say much on our drive to the Sky Harbor Airport, the car could barely contain our excitement. In the hangar, I watched in silent admiration as Joan went through her inspection of the rented Cessna. When she was satisfied with her preliminary inspection, we rolled the plane out on the runway and soon we were on board with Joan going through her preflight checklist. Through the years we never ran out of subjects to talk about, but today would be different. Determined that I would say nothing to distract her from the business of flying, I had forgotten that the engine drone was an effective deterrent to conversation. I watched every move as she skillfully guided the rented Cessna down the runway and up, up above the trees and power lines out over St. Louis Bay.

This was the best adventure we had shared in our years of friendship. We had left the cares of the world behind us, and we grinned at one another like kids who had put one over on the grownups. The water and landscape below us spread out in miniature, our own special gameboard over which we skipped along never losing our turn at the dice. A toy Aerial Bridge connected the finger of Park Point with its sandy beach bisecting Lake Superior and St. Louis Bay, then on above the tiny stacks of elevators and geometric patches of spring green land and deep blue water. We made the circle over the St. Louis River winding its way below the hills surrounding the city.

Back to the landing area, the circle completed, Joan triumphantly brought our little craft to a perfect landing. On the ground, we exchanged the thoughts that had crossed our minds during the flight. Joan confided that she kept thinking how she had taken my life in her hands and was gratified by my complete trust in her. I hoped her sense of responsibility for me had not overshadowed the joy of her accomplishment, and I responded:

"I never doubted you would be a great pilot. I'm not surprised you made a perfect landing."

With typical modesty she replied, "Thanks, but I have to admit this plane is pretty easy to land. It has a back wheel that adds to stability during landing. The plane I usually fly had only the two front wheels."

A few years later I would fly with her in her own Piper Cub, again accomplishing a perfect landing, but this time on floats on Gull Wing Lake in Ontario, Canada. Having her own plane was a joy beyond her dreams, and her appreciation of it has never diminished. Though it has been a number of years since that first flight, when my mind replays the experience, my heart is warmed by the unique pleasure of sharing in the fruition of a friend's cherished dream.

∾

Sixty-Something
at the Clinic

*A*t a certain age, I began spending many hours at the eye clinic waiting for Hartley while he received what seemed to be endless hours of examinations and preparation for eye surgery related to diabetes. I tried to pass the time reading and writing, but sometimes the conversations in the waiting room were too distracting to concentrate. One day I found myself listening with amusement and finally recording, in shorthand, the conversation I overheard. This is how it went:

"Hullo Matt, where you been keepin' yourself?" The speaker was a stocky man in a windbreaker jacket and red baseball cap.

"Well, if it ain't Joe! By golly, it's been a long time. I don't think I've seen you since you retired."

"How you been anyway, Matt? You here for a checkup?"

"Not doin' so good the last few years. That prostate trouble kept gettin' worse. I finally had to have an operation and I'm still feelin' poor. It sure ain't no fun gettin' old."

"You know, Matt I just ignore all the things people our age complain about. I keep on goin' along and don't give in to every little thing other people run to doctors for. I brought the wife in today to get her eyes checked. She thinks she needs new glasses. Me, I just go to Walgreen's and pick out a pair that feels good. They work fine for me."

"Ya," Matt said, "I brought the wife in for her checkup today too."

"I forgot to ask you. How's Sophie doin'?"

"Not so good. She had cancer, you know. She was laid up for a long time after her operation, and hasn't been able to do much around the house since. Makes it that much harder for me. Seems like the minute you retire, your health goes. I guess that's life."

"Matt, it's all in your head. You got to forget about your age. I just get up in the morning, and if I don't see my name in the funeral notices, I figure I'm in good shape. I put my aches and pains out of my mind and go about my business."

"Maybe that works for you, Joe, but it's getting so my joints hurt so bad I can barely get out of bed in the morning. Then when I do, I can hardly bend over to tie my shoes. What I wouldn't give to be thirty again!"

When Joe replied, his voice had lost some of his conviction, "Well, Matt, maybe I have been slowin' down a little too the past few years. I only planted half my garden this year. We can't use all that produce anymore. Of course, we can give it to the kids, but they aren't willin' to help with any of the plantin' or weedin', even though it's killin' my back to do it. They don't seem to appreciate it anyhow. Maybe next year I'll just forget the garden."

With a tug on his baseball cap, Joe paused before he continued,

"You know, we keep hearing about *The Golden Years*. I should be puttin' my feet up and enjoyin' life. If only I felt better, maybe I could enjoy my retirement. I tell you, Matt, I'd like to get ahold of the guy who started calling these *The Golden Years*. I swear I'd strangle him!"

❧

Y2K

December 30, 1999, Journal Entry

When did we stop referring to the year two thousand as the "turn of the century" or "end of the millennium" and begin talking about Y2K? It must have been about the time a few years back when it was revealed that through a ghastly oversight, the world's computer systems were not prepared to advance into the twenty first century. The great minds of the industry had put us in cyberspace, but somehow had failed to look far enough ahead to carry us beyond 1999. The task is now a race with time to make our computers "Y2K compliant" (a phrase which has become hackneyed in the past few months) before midnight tomorrow, December 31, 1999.

John Koskinen, appointed by President Clinton as Special Coordinator of the United States' effort in the race, assures us we have every reason to be confident that the transition into 2000 will be made smoothly and without incident.

I must confess, I am secretly pleased by the unseasonably warm weather in Duluth. In the event of power/gas/water or communications failure, we should manage to keep from freezing. Recalling a storm some years ago that caused a three-day power outage with the fireplace our only source of heat, I'm regretting the decision to convert the fireplace to gas. I have the usual food supplies on hand, adequate to provide balanced meals for several days.

Though I'm counting on the brilliant mind power and billions of dollars invested in the great Y2K race to prevent major breakdowns of services, there are two other specters looming on the horizon which are unsettling to all of us in varying degrees. First, threats of terrorist acts in locations around the world. Second, we have a number of self-appointed soothsayers predicting the destruction of the planet at the end of the millennium.

Terrorist threats cannot be discounted. The horror of the Oklahoma City Federal Building bombing continues to cast a shadow over the country. Car, airplane, and embassy bombings occur internationally with alarming frequency. Many Y2K special events are planned throughout the nation and the world to be attended by millions of citizens. I pray for the safety of all the world's celebrants.

The dire predictions of mankind's demise are dismissed out-of-hand by most of us. Doomsday people emerge on every momentous occasion to claim direct communication with God and warn the world accordingly that the end is near.

The media hyperbole seems to exacerbate expectations of doom to a point where the scales could be tipped to produce extreme reactions by the public, creating needless shortages and communication overloads. I wonder if perhaps the real race is not between the programming experts and the clock, but between the media glut of hysteria-producing speculation and the ability of the populace to remain rational in their thinking and controlled in their actions. Considering this, I will be happy to see the end of 1999.

December 31, 1999, Journal Entry

The moment of truth is at hand. The last day of the century has dawned clear with record-setting high temperatures. The newspapers and television are full of Y2K reports and speculation. The Mayor of Seattle has announced the cancellation of his city's New Year's Eve celebration due to evidence of planned terrorist activity. Other cities, including New York, will increase security and protective measures, but hold their celebrations as planned. I approve of this refusal to be held hostage by terrorists. New York is expecting two million people in Times Square at midnight, twice the usual New Year's gathering.

Local authorities continue to report that the City of Duluth is prepared for the turn of the century. Yet, as the day wears on, a certain apprehension creeps into my expectation of a smooth Y2K entry. I have a reasonable supply of water prepared for emergency use and a number of candles at hand in case of power failure. We can't imagine living on hoarded supplies while our neighbors go without, so we do not add to our modest larder.

This morning as I return from an errand, Marnie calls from her porch next door, "Are you ready for Y2K?"

I reply that I have some wonderful peaches I canned in September that we can share to spark up cold meals if things get too bad. As we laugh together, I think how blessed we are to have Marnie, Peter and their two children, along with their dog and two cats, living next door.

Preparing for the care of our own two cats, Pearl and Sam, amounts to nothing more than checking the level of their "scientifically developed" diet food, kitty litter and extra water. I smile at the thought of the simplicity of their basic needs. They are far better equipped to cope with loss of physical comforts than we are. I have read that cats are the pets best suited to move comfortably from their natural outdoor habitat to indoor human environments with easy adaptability. While in our human world, Pearl and Sam do require, in addition to their physical needs, a certain amount of companionship and shows of affection from us.

Hartley is ill, and we agree it is a good plan to celebrate at home this year. We are cheered by our seafood dinner and early reports from other time zones around the world on the lack of computer glitches or terrorist attacks on celebrants. We watch telecasts of spectacular fireworks as the great cities of the world light up the sky to mark the occasion. A report from Kosovo where skies remain dark serves as a grim reminder that United Nations troops continue struggling to maintain their peace-keeping vigil, seemingly to no avail.

In recent years, Hartley and I have slept right through the arrival of the new year, but midnight, 1999 finds us wide awake to watch the safe and triumphant entry of Y2K at Times Square teeming with its two million revelers. This is my last journal entry of the millennium.

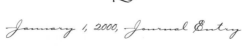

January 1, 2000, Journal Entry

Though we have yet to experience our first business day of 2000 on January 3rd, we have survived entry into the new millennium. I pour out the containers of water and put away the candles. Today, we are reading and hearing stories of extreme survival tactics undertaken by area residents that they now regret. One person is being treated at Miller Dwan Burn Center for injuries suffered when he tried to test-start a generator purchased to be used in the event of power failure. Other stories tell about hoarding of food and other supplies, and building and stocking survival shelters. One family had spent $20,000 on supplies and now wonders how to recover some of its investment. The hoarding of food does offer an opportunity for donations to the needy through the area's food shelf program.

January 6, 2000, Journal Entry

The first business day of the millennium has brought forth a few glitches in computer services, perhaps causing some minor inconvenience. The stock market has not collapsed and some people are wondering what all the fuss was about, but the majority of us seem to believe the fuss was warranted to avert potential disaster.

I wonder if, at a date in the future, someone will read this account of Y2K and say laughingly (if the terminology is still relevant), "That was back in the early days of cybernation when computer technology was in its infancy."

Part Five:

Bread Pudding

Messenger
Unaware

etween 1996 and 2004, I experienced an unusual number of challenges. Hartley and I alternated with hospital stays involving life-threatening illness, our home was destroyed by fire, and Hartley died only months after the fire. Throughout these years, people frequently asked me where I found the strength to sustain me through these traumas.

In looking back over the years, I saw the beginning as a time in 1995 when I received a magnificent spiritual gift from a friend named Patricia McDunough that helped prepare me for the difficult times I would soon face. She was, of course, unaware that she was helping to define the person I would become in later years.

In reading a book by Bishop Desmond Tutu called *God Has a Dream,* I found a passage which suggested that one way to begin cultivating the ability to love is to see yourself as a center of love, an oasis of peace, as a pool of serenity with ripples going out to all those around you.

These qualities were conveyed by Pat, and though she is gone, her gift continues to nourish many souls as those ripples are passed on by people whose lives she touched.

In 1995, I was a little past sixty and beginning to realize that my retirement years were fast approaching. I wondered how I could be of service to other people during those years. I felt a need to give something back to a world that had richly blessed me.

It was in this climate of thinking that I became reacquainted with Patricia. I had seen her often in my early years, then less frequently as time moved on. She was in her early eighties when I learned that she had undergone throat surgery that disfigured her face, robbed her of her ability to speak, and required her to eat only pureed food. After intensive therapy to regain her speech, she returned to her home where family members looked in on her daily.

One evening I was invited to a gathering where Pat was also a guest. It was the first time I had seen her since her surgery and I was apprehensive. But as I looked into those sapphire blue eyes, still bright and sparkling with the joy of living, I forgot the damaged face. I saw only gracious acceptance in her manner. We had a good talk and agreed that I would come to see her the next week.

And so our visits began. I brought a new variety of homemade soup each time, thinking soup was nourishing and not too bad pureed. She was enthusiastic and had not lost her sense of humor. Yet there was a certain peaceful aura about her of courage and serenity that I knew was rooted in faith. She was a devout Catholic, but we did not discuss religious matters. We just talked and the hours flew. I had started these visits to brighten the long winter days for Pat, but soon discovered I was receiving a precious gift, along with a new perspective on my upcoming retirement.

Our visits continued into early spring, and then one day Pat died. She just...died. I was terribly saddened, yet I knew she was well-prepared to die, and we had certainly made the most of our time together. Reflecting on our visits, it seemed that the serenity centering her life had enabled her to just get on with the process of living, making each day count. I knew then that whatever the future held for me, I wanted to live the rest of my life in a manner that would allow me to die well as Pat had done.

I could not know how soon I would be calling on her example of faith and courage to help see me through a long series of troubles in my life.

About two months after Pat's death, I awoke one morning struggling to breathe and was rushed off to the hospital. Certain I was dying, I was relieved to learn that replacement of a heart valve would correct my problem. But at 11 P.M. alone and sleepless, relief quickly gave way to panic as I thought of the two weeks looming ahead before the surgery. I had never been ill before, and the idea of heart surgery was terrifying. I prayed earnestly for strength and courage. I didn't want to add my fear to my family's concern for me. Finally I said almost angrily, "God, I give up. I don't know how to do this, I don't need this—I'm giving it to you to figure out!"

That said, my burden lightened considerably. I opened my heart and mind, and waited. The answer to my prayer was simple and came within minutes, although it was not quite what I expected. I hadn't thought of Pat in those first few days of anxiety, but now my mind was flooded with the legacy of strength and faith she had left for me to draw on. I was suddenly well aware that, in my place, Pat would simply take hold and prepare for surgery, as I now resolved to do. It was as if she had provided a how-to list for me to prepare myself, and I was confident I could manage it. Above all, I would assure my family that God was in charge so they need not worry.

In the weeks that followed, whenever my courage began to flag, I thought of how Pat dealt with her illness. The seed she had planted continued to grow and strengthen me to later face those problems yet to come. She seemed to be God's messenger sent to illuminate my path. That path has led me on a different journey than I had planned for my retirement, but it has been a journey filled with blessings.

∾

The Skywalk
Challenge

ow quickly it seemed our lives had changed. We thought we would go on indefinitely skiing the Rockies in winter and walking the eighteen fairways of Lester Park Golf Course in summer. Then one year, we found ourselves spending an alarming number of our days in hospitals and clinic waiting rooms among people we believed to be much older than ourselves.

It seemed to just happen overnight, but in reality, a few years had slipped away before Hartley's walking had become impaired by the effects of diabetes. I had made two trips to heart surgery and was now, once again slowed by the symptoms of heart failure. For a time we had kidded one another into believing we would be returning to our old selves before long. On April 14, 2001, the day before Easter, we celebrated our fiftieth wedding anniversary. By then we were beginning to realize it was time to acknowledge that those old selves were behind us. We were learning to make adjustments for the limitations presented by our new selves.

Two days after Easter, I answered an early-morning phone call from Aftenro Home where Hartley's ninety five year old father lived. The caller gently informed me that Dad had passed away in the night. In the next few days, we managed to sandwich funeral arrangements and the disposition of Dad's belongings between tests I was undergoing in anticipation of my third heart surgery.

The day of the funeral Hartley and I left the reception early for a consultation with Dr. Wickstrom, my cardiac surgeon, to discuss scheduling of the heart operation. I had mustered up my courage and was determined to get on his surgery schedule at the earliest open date before my resolve failed me.

"Perfect weather for a funeral," I observed as we hurried through the wind and rain.

The demands of the day had taken their toll on us and we arrived frazzled and breathless at the reception desk of St. Mary's new Cardiac Care Center. We were dismayed to learn that my surgeon was still using his old office on the other side of the complex, a skywalk away. For a moment we were crestfallen at the prospect of the long hike, but we soon rallied and even began to laugh at ourselves as we approached the skywalk.

"Aren't we a pair! Well, we can just walk slowly and rest often," I told Hartley.

I thought of the years we had routinely covered miles of golf course fairways in record time. Now we were challenged by a walk amounting to perhaps two blocks.

The second or third time we stopped to rest, Hartley began to grumble, "Why are wheelchairs for patient use sitting around everywhere, except when you really need one?"

"It doesn't matter; I don't think I'd have the strength to push you if we could locate one," I replied.

He shot me a strange, startled look. "Are you kidding? I was talking about pushing you."

With that we lapsed into helpless laughter at ourselves, the situation, and life itself. Our rest stops became more frequent throughout the remainder of our trek as we collapsed with laughter against the sides of the skywalk whenever we caught sight of someone being pushed in a wheelchair.

∾

Where Were You When...?

heard the unmistakable sound of a helicopter in the distance and left my bed to look out the window of my seventh floor room where I watched the blinking lights approaching as the chopper circled to land on the hospital roof. I said a silent prayer for the passenger being rushed to surgery or the emergency room, hoping that their treatment would be successful. It was nearly dawn now and the first grey light began creeping across the sky. Good; at least I would soon have some human contact. The bloodletters came early, around 5 A.M., their arrival heralded by the rattle of their metal carts well-stocked with needles, swabs, and little vials designed to gobble up patients' blood. This was done as early as possible each day to obtain lab results before the doctors arrived to begin their rounds.

I had been fortunate to spend little time in hospitals until I was past sixty. My first experience with heart surgery gave me a fascinating insight into the world of caregivers and patients. I had plenty of time to contemplate the amazing technology and dedicated people inhabiting this place that seemed like a small planet unto itself. I surprised myself by embracing the experience rather than simply tolerating it, which was the best I had hoped for. As I began to recover, I spent time in waiting areas talking to visitors who were often frightened, anxious to see their loved ones between tests and treatments. Many were from outlying areas in Minnesota, Wisconsin, or Michigan, staying in a strange city with no other family nearby. They were grateful to talk to a local resident who could answer their questions about the city and the hospital.

As time went on, I had two more heart surgeries, the third just four months ago in May of 2001. Now I was here on the third day of my third hospital stay since that surgery. It hadn't been a good summer, and it was likely that I would still be here six days from now for my sixty eighth birthday on September seventeenth. I sighed with resignation as I heard the phlebotomist's cart coming down the hall, but smiled as I recognized the young woman who rolled the cart into my room. She was one of the good ones. I was known as a "hard draw," yet she deftly slipped the needle in and drew her sample with no fuss, pleased that she had wielded her needle without causing pain.

I steeled myself for the next two hours between dawn and breakfast, which were the longest and loneliest of the day. I would soon have reason to wish the hours had stretched out into just another boring day in a long hospital stay.

Mary, my new roommate, woke early and turned on her television. She proved to be pleasant, and we visited through breakfast, though I found the television annoying. After breakfast, I was reading the morning paper when Mary suddenly shouted, "An airplane just hit a building! It's not a movie! It's really happening!"

The television now had my full attention. It was about 8:45 and we were horrified as we watched a news bulletin replay of an airliner striking a tall building, which I now recognized as the World Trade Center in New York City. As the plane exploded on contact, black smoke poured from a gaping hole and enveloped the upper floors. Shock and confusion combined to nearly immobilize us. We still were looking at it as a horrible accident, when other reports began to come through and make some inroads into our stunned disbelief. It was possible that this was a terrorist attack.

By now, other people were coming into the room, nursing staff and housekeepers clustered around the television. The world seemed to stand still except for the terrible events playing out on the screen. Suddenly another plane appeared on the scene before us. Was it a replay? No, there was the gaping hole in the north tower and this plane was headed directly for the south tower. We watched the second plane strike, sickened as we realized this could not be accidental. It was about 9 A.M. The hospital staff members began to back away and take care of their duties with one eye on the screen, realizing that this small world of St. Mary's Hospital could not be allowed to grind to a halt. They had patients and rooms to care for, and so they did. September eleventh was giving me yet another window through which to view the hospital operation.

My first thought was, "How do I get out of here? I can't just lie here doing nothing!"

I had to talk to Hartley. Had he been watching? He did not have the television on when I called, and sounded as confused as I felt at the first news. He was anxious to get off the phone and see firsthand what was happening, then he would get down to the hospital as soon as he could. By now, all cities were taking stock of their own situations to determine what locations might be targeted in their area, should this prove to be a widespread attack. My doctors made their morning calls, and spoke of the tragic events unfolding, watching the latest reports between their patient care duties. It was surreal, as though these people should not have to be wielding stethoscopes and taking pulses when the world was falling apart. Many business places could simply close if they were disposed to do so, but this business of healing couldn't be put on hold. My cardiologist was in Chicago for the day speaking at a seminar. I wondered when he would get back, or how. Now all air traffic in the country was grounded.

I thought of my son and his wife on a vacation trip to Canada, and my sister-in-law and her husband in England. How sad for them to be away from the country hearing the awful news. I learned from them later that people in their host countries had been of great comfort to them.

My roommate was from a small Minnesota town and her husband was planning to drive to Duluth that evening to visit her. She called to tell him not to leave the children to make the trip. She thought it was more important for him to stay with them.

Hartley came to visit and we continued to follow with increasing horror the stories of the losses that were mounting up as the day wore on. We learned of a third plane attacking the Pentagon. Next we heard of a plane over Pennsylvania, whose passengers were making contact via cell phones with people on the ground saying they had been skyjacked and were hostages of terrorists who planned to use their plane as a weapon to attack the White House. The passengers told of plans to rush the terrorists and crash the plane since they knew they were doomed in any case. The plane crashed in an unpopulated area as their heroic plan succeeded.

Other heroes would die in the collapse of the Trade Center towers. By 10:30 A.M. both towers had come down in a pile of rubble taking with them about two thousand office workers and hundreds of firefighters and police. The devastation extended far beyond the trade towers. The sky was filled with grey ash which obscured the sun and covered the streets for many city blocks. A number of homes and business places in the area had to be abandoned due to damage and contamination. When Hartley left, I escaped from replays of earlier news reports to walk in the halls.

The visitors' solarium was occupied with people glued to the television screen. I could get away from the screens, but not the sounds. Every room had a television set on as I walked in the corridor, and there was no respite from the repeated horror. Sometime in the afternoon, I found the solarium empty with television blaring. I turned it off, and had the first quiet moment I had experienced since 8:45 that morning.

I returned to my room for dinner to find the local news was airing. A familiar scene flashed on the screen, the interior of First Lutheran Church, my church. People were gathering there for prayer and comfort. I saw my friends drawing together, and longed to be there with them. It cheered me to see them, but it accentuated my loneliness. During the evening I heard sniffles from Mary's bed. I knew she was crying, and I inquired if I could help her. She was scared and lonely and wishing she had not told her husband to stay home. I felt far less sorry for myself after considering her situation. She was truly isolated from home and family.

We faced the new day with dread. It seemed so long since I watched September eleventh dawn. My cardiologist was one of the first doctors to visit me that next day. He sat down in the chair by my bed and told me of a Chicago with streets patrolled by the National Guard. Everyone was leaving downtown, and no one was allowed to come into that area after the attack on New York. Dr. Rich had attended medical school in Chicago so it was a familiar city to him, but now it appeared to be an occupied city in a war zone. All he could think of was getting home to his family. He couldn't use his plane ticket, of course, but the concierge at his hotel managed to get him a car, a near impossibility after the airports closed. As he talked, I wondered what precautions had been taken in Minneapolis where my daughter lives. My sister had arrived in Duluth on September tenth from Rochester, N. Y. She had decided to come when she learned I was hospitalized again. Now we wondered if she would be able to get back to her family on schedule.

As this day progressed, we began to learn of more heroic efforts to save lives and ease suffering. Many people were heading for New York from all over the U.S. to assist in search and rescue and the grim task of retrieving the dead. There was hope and a sense of community that many Americans had believed was lost. Cynics seemed to be subdued by the outpouring of goodwill and donations of monetary aid that came forth following the cruel and unprovoked attack. It would take many weeks for the enormity of the atrocity to be realized, and life in these United States would never again be the same as it was before September 11, 2001.

❧

Burnout

stood with Hartley on the front sidewalk watching in helpless shock as a crew of valiant Duluth firefighters struggled to contain the fire that was rapidly consuming our home. It was just after noon on the first warm day of 2003, April fourteenth, our fifty second wedding anniversary.

News spread, along with the fire, and more people arrived on the scene. Most of them came to offer help, bringing cell phones, cold beverages, and invitations into their homes. Even strangers who joined the group offered their prayers and sympathy, rather than simply gawking.

Noise emanating from the three fire trucks parked on the street made use of the proffered cell phones nearly impossible, but by moving down the street, we managed to hear well enough to contact our children and other family members to let them know we were safely outside the inferno.

The acrid smoke affronting our nostrils told us that carpeting and upholstery were rapidly turning into charred rubble. The destructive force seemed to be measured by its own pulse and rhythm that kept beat with the sound of the shiny red equipment. Firefighters worked as one, straining to win the battle against flame and smoke. I prayed for their safety as leaded windows smashed to the floor joining my treasured paintings and mirrors.

My precious Chickering baby grand piano sat in the front alcove of the living room. The fire had started in the rear of the house. Maybe, oh maybe, somehow it would survive, but I could almost hear the greedy flames declaring a special taste for old ivory and mellow mahogany as they roared through the living room. Why had I left the lid up? The keyboard cover was not closed either. I pictured the sheet music curling at the edges before bursting into flame and quickly disintegrating under the brooding stare of the Beethoven bust sitting to the right of the music rack. What piece had I been playing only this morning before my life was turned upside down?

The worst was finally over; the fire had ripped from the rear deck and sunroom to the front of the house in about fifteen minutes. A firefighter approached me, and I had to ask, "What about the piano?"

He shook his head sadly.

"Do you have some place you could stay for a while?" he asked.

It had already been determined that we would stay with my sister, who had been with me through most of the fire. I was suddenly overwhelmed by the realization that we were homeless.

Crew members were now asking if I wanted them to go in and try to recover valuables before the house was boarded up and secured. No, I didn't want anyone to return to that smoking ruin.

"How about jewelry? That sometimes survives. Just tell us where to look."

I told him, and he was back in a few minutes, white teeth flashing a grin through the grime and sweat lining his face. He was carrying my wooden jewelry box, black and charred now, but with the contents intact.

"Is there anything else we can look for?" another crew member asked.

It finally dawned on me that my writing was all contained in my study above the living room. I had not taken my son's sound advice to store discs of my writing in the safe deposit box. Surely it was beyond hope of recovery. When I mentioned this, I was cheered by her reply.

"That room received the least damage. Let me look."

I described the binders to look for, and she was off. She returned shortly, and I could see by the triumphant smile above the binders she carried that the pages were legible. There was no way to thank these gallant and gracious people.

The fire chief came to sit beside me on the steps of our neighbor's house which had been our gathering place for the afternoon. Placing a gentle hand on my shoulder he said, "It will get better. I know it doesn't seem that way now, but I promise you, it will be better. Try to remember that."

How kind he had been, along with his entire crew. I tried to believe him.

Someone suggested I leave now with my sister. My husband and son would remain until the house was secured. I picked up a bag of clothing my friend and neighbor had provided to tide me over.

"You can't possibly put on those same clothes tomorrow," she had said.

I felt as burned out and empty as the house which had been our home for thirty nine years. I turned away from the scene and followed my sister to her car without looking back.

Aftermath

Armed with plastic bags and flashlights, we approached the silent ruin that had been our home the day before. I tried to avoid looking at the front lawn where a pile of burned trash which had graced our living room as furniture was now mercilessly exposed to the sputtering rain and angry winds off Lake Superior. The unseasonably warm mid-April weather had given way to that more appropriate for a Duluth spring. The temperature had dropped thirty degrees overnight, and gale force winds were predicted for the next three days.

Mentally noting that the weather matched my state of mind perfectly, I addressed my two children in a brusque voice not quite my own,

"Let's get on with it."

We were seeking safe deposit box keys and papers related to taxes. We also hoped to make a quick survey to see if there were any mementos worth trying to salvage. My husband was too ill to accompany us on our grim errand.

The fire marshall had given us permission to enter the house, but warned us not to stay inside for very long at a time.

"The air inside the house contains toxic materials, and it will be dangerous to breathe in there for any length of time," he advised us.

The front steps were concrete, and so remained intact. A small familiar-shaped piece of antique pottery stood on the top step. It had been one of my favorite pieces, but now its beautiful turquoise glaze was an ugly dull black. With an effort, I restrained my sudden impulse to pick it up and fling it against the steps to complete its destruction lest I be tempted to consider the possibility of salvage.

My son Hartley struggled with the lock, which finally responded to his efforts. As the door opened, we were assailed by an overwhelming stench

which I could never have imagined. It almost sent me reeling back. For a
moment I wasn't sure I could manage to enter, but forced myself to step
inside. I had the sense of entering a tomb. An all-pervasive damp and freezing chill enveloped us and hastened us along on our mission. Our flashlights
were a poor substitute for natural light now obliterated by slabs of hastily
nailed up plywood that replaced the windows.

Perhaps it is merciful that we had such meager light to view the rubble
that had been carpeting, mirrors, paintings, and treasured heirlooms from
previous generations of our families. Although the fire chief had told me it
was beyond salvation, I had to turn my flashlight on my beloved baby grand,
an old irreplaceable Chickering. I was compelled to press a key, but even
though a sound came forth, I could see it was hopeless.

Over it all, the wretched smell clung, to our clothing and everything we
tried to salvage. We finally located the safe deposit box keys on the floor near
my small antique desk, now burned almost beyond recognition. Everything
was coated with a black sticky substance that we weren't sure was removable.
We found few of the sought-after papers, but bagged in plastic the few
things we deemed candidates for salvage. We made mental notes of other
items we spotted to remove on our next trip.

I soon came to realize that the indescribable smell was comprised of
burned wood, paper, plaster, plastic, foam rubber, carpeting, upholstery,
leather, rubber, chemicals, varnish, paint, and every other product found in
a household. It all combined to produce the sticky tar-like substance covering everything.

Some days later, I was seeking a new computer to replace my writing
equipment which had melted in the fire. The young man who was helping
me, asked what I had been using previously. My old equipment was, of
course, familiar and very satisfactory, but now obsolete and no longer available. He was curious about my replacing something that was working so
well for me. When we told him it had melted in a house fire, he simply said,
"I will never forget that smell as long as I live. Have you ever smelled anything worse?"

His home had burned when he was six years old, and the smell was his
most vivid memory of the event, as I expect it will be for me.

∾

Binding the Wounds

*M*arch is my least favorite month in Duluth. This year of 2004, it accentuated the feeling of emptiness in my heart and home following the death of my husband on February twenty sixth. For most of the three weeks Hartley was hospitalized, our daughter Dawn, who lives in New Brighton, stayed with me and had remained for a few days following the funeral.

Our efforts those days to begin acknowledging the many communications and kindnesses we had received were half-hearted and usually ended with our dissolving into tears, clinging together for comfort. The weather continued to be less than pleasant, and evenings felt chilly even indoors.

On one of those evenings, Dawn was casting about for a warm shirt or sweater, when I recalled the soft, warm shirts I had purchased for Hartley to wear on his trips to chemotherapy during the winter. There were two, one blue and one tan. The blue one matched Dawn's eyes. I took it from the hanger and handed it to her. She pulled it on gratefully.

"It feels so nice; almost like Dad is giving me a hug."

I suggested she take it home and wear it around the house or for a nightshirt when she needed comfort. She thought I might need it for comfort, but I assured her I would wear the tan shirt. And so we clung to our comforting shirts using them to begin binding our wounds.

The articles of clothing worn by Hartley were limited. Last year in April, when our home was destroyed by fire, our clothing went with it. Hartley was ill for most of the nine months he had lived in our new home, so was often clad in night clothes. Most of the newly purchased clothing remained in his closet and had no connection with Hartley.

We had been fortunate to move into the one remaining apartment in a new building close to our ruined home. This is a more suitable residence for me as I continue my life journey alone, yet I was sad to have few mementos of Hartley to give his loved ones. I discovered his grandfather's gold watch in the safe deposit box. Good, this was intended for our son. Dawn has her grandmother's wedding ring, but what did I have of her father's to give her? I had a money clip I had given him many years ago and he loved it. It was well-worn and a perfect talisman for Dawn. I didn't think she would use it as a money clip, but perhaps it might hold papers on her desk.

The week of April eleventh, Dawn returned to Duluth for a visit. It was the week of Hartley's birthday and our fifty third wedding anniversary, which was also the anniversary of our house fire. She thought I would appreciate her company during that week, and she was right. I noticed she wore the blue shirt for a nightshirt, and on our first shopping trip, she pulled the money clip from her pocket to pay for her purchase. We are beginning to heal.

❧

Where Did Donna Go?

When our home was destroyed by fire in April of 2003, Hartley and I tried to be philosophical, grateful that the fire occurred at noon rather than midnight. We went about furnishing our new apartment in the Lakeside Apartments just completed that winter. People came forward to help, often bearing gifts. The daily shopping trips proved to be hard work, as neither of us was in good health. We laughingly said, "We don't buy green bananas, but here we are buying an apartment full of new furniture."

Yet, we actually had fun remembering our shopping trips together over fifty years earlier to furnish our first apartment. There was a lot of bantering during our almost daily stops at Marshall's Hardware store. We had been customers for the fifty years we lived in Lakeside, and the staff jokingly likened us to a couple of college kids setting up an off-campus apartment.

"What are you kids looking for today?" someone would ask.

"I suppose you'll need to get set up for those wild parties you'll be throwing."

Everywhere in our community we received encouragement, goodwill, and support, and after all, we still had each other.

By July, we were fairly well settled into our new home, but Hartley's health was rapidly deteriorating. The lymphoma which had seemingly been in remission returned with a vengeance. Now the shopping days gave way to rounds of tests, doctor appointments, and months of chemotherapy. Between treatments, we managed to squeeze in completion of insurance claims and the sale of the remains of our property.

In February we were back at the hospital for what proved to be Hartley's final illness. His suffering and our life together ended with his death on

February twenty sixth. Why is it we never quite believe someone can leave us until that moment when they are no more?

I busied myself in my attractive new surroundings answering letters of condolence and sending thank you cards for flowers and memorials. I resumed the previously abandoned shopping trips to complete decoration of my strangely silent home and thought I was beginning to feel comfortable there. As summer approached and the numbing grief began to ebb at times, I discovered my energy level was increasing. I was beginning to return to life, but starting to wonder who I was. Who was this strange woman living in this strange new place wearing unfamiliar clothing?

I had had no qualms about giving away Hartley's barely worn clothing, most of which had been hastily chosen and purchased by my daughter and me, but was dismayed that there seemed to be nothing left of Hartley's to give his children as keepsakes—until I thought of the safe deposit box. I was gratified to find something special for each of our family members, comforted by finding these small tokens.

As I moved into fall and winter, I was more mentally alert and physically stronger, but less sure who I was. The loss of our personal belongings became more devastating than it had been the day of the fire. Nothing remained but the stories I had written and my jewelry, which the firefighters had salvaged for me. Now the stories seemed to have been written by someone else. It was as if all evidence of the person I had been was erased. Suddenly everything around me seemed foreign and it was finally sinking in that Hartley was never coming back.

"I must learn to look at this as an opportunity to reinvent Donna," I told myself. Perhaps it is just as well that I have few faded photos and tired mementos of the past to brood over. I don't really need that outdated material evidence to affirm my existence, do I? Then on Valentine's Day I received a shipment of books containing the first story I have had published. As I took a book from the box, I smiled remembering how pleased Hartley was the day I received the publisher's galley pages of my story. I was grateful Hartley was still here to share that moment with me. The books could not have come at a better time. Their arrival seemed to mark the beginning of a new place in the world for me where I can treasure the best of the past through my stories while I move forward to discover the new Donna.

∾

Emergence; Moving On

It is All Saint's Day, 2004. This morning we light candles in church to celebrate the lives of loved ones who have passed on. It is eight months since Hartley died and recently I have noticed that the protective numbness which accompanies loss, seems to be wearing away. I am coming to terms with the new direction my life has taken, or am I?

I manage to maintain my composure during the service, but as I drive out of the church parking lot, the hot tears spill over, scalding my cheeks. He can't really be gone, I think, but worse, why does the pain still strike anew, as though I just heard the news. Haven't I known it all these months?

I had begun to emerge from the pall of grief in recent weeks and was becoming aware that I am alive again. Now it seems that awareness comes with a price that is exacted by these moments of relapse. In spite of the preparation offered by dear friends who have lost their husbands, I am taken unaware by my feelings and realize I have a long way to go in this business of healing. I can stop my car, return to the church and find solace among those friends. But the deadly sin of pride, one of my failings, dictates that I must be strong and keep this lapse of control to myself.

At home, I assemble ingredients to make beef barley soup and homemade bread. That will occupy at least part of the day. I'm learning to keep my hands busy and hope the mind will follow. But more importantly, I am starting to overcome the inertia that has held me in its grip these past eight months and manage to accomplish at least some of the tasks I set out for myself.

The aroma of rising bread lifts my spirits. I'll make two loaves and freeze one. The soup is another matter. How long will I be eating this, I wonder.

Diet restrictions preclude indulging in a generous bowl, allowing instead a stingy cup. Ah, just one of the ironies that accompany the process of aging. I laugh in spite of myself. As I move to the living room to spend an hour at the piano while the bread rises, I find myself thinking that I won't have any trouble finding a friend who'll be glad to share homemade soup.

I will get through this day somehow.... And another... And another.

Randi's Legacy

On Friday morning, April 28, 2006, the mailcarrier knocked on my apartment door to deliver a package. It was about eight inches square and was wrapped in brown paper. It was hand-addressed to Donna and Hartley Schilling at our old address. The return address was from someone I did not know in St. Peter, Minnesota.

Anyone who knows us is aware that our home had been destroyed by fire three years ago, and Hartley had died within months of our move to this apartment. Obviously, the sender was a stranger to us, and I began to think about the mail bombs and anthrax mailings with bogus return addresses that had plagued the country in recent years. I wondered what precautions I should take before opening it. Finally I gingerly slit open one bottom edge. This revealed an envelope attached to the cardboard box inside. The envelope contained the following letter:

Dear Schillings, Lafaye Heieie, who was my aunt died in Sioux Falls on February 7 of this year at age eighty six years.

I was named executor of her estate and have been going through her things. Among them I found the box with her note on it about who should receive the butter mold. It looks very interesting and I wonder just how it was used. In any case I had no idea who "Donna and Hartley" were until I recently found an envelope with I'm assuming, your address on it. At least I hope it is you, and if not, perhaps you might know to whom it belongs.

All my best, Ranae Peterson

My mind raced back about sixty years to the time my mother was placed on a salt-free diet. Salt-free butter was not readily available, so Mother cleverly made her own by beating cream in the electric mixer. She explained that butter-making was one of the chores assigned to her on the family farm near Greenbush, Minnesota.

She went on to tell us about the beautiful butter mold into which she pressed the freshly-churned butter. She described the mold as wooden and round with a hole in the top through which a handle was inserted. There was a round flat wooden piece attached to the bottom of the handle and hand carved with acorns and leaves. When the butter was turned out on a dish, this design appeared on top.

Now, holding the package, I was really excited. Could it possibly contain my grandmother, Randi Heieie's butter mold? I eagerly tore off the remaining wrappings, and there on the side of the box was a tag fastened with tape yellowed with age with this message:

> *"Save for: Hartley and Donna Schilling.*
> *This is your Grandmother's butter mold."*

I lifted the lid of the box and pulled out the wooden mold worn satin-smooth from years of use and yes, there were the acorns and leaves. On the handle, the year 1870 was inscribed, which led me to believe Randi's mother, my Great Grandmother Odden must have used it before giving it to her daughter. My grandmother was not married until 1884.

LaFaye was the wife of my Uncle Marion Heieie, Mother's only brother and the last member of Mother's family to die. He left us in 2004. How dear LaFaye and her niece were to safeguard this family treasure and find a way to send it to us.

It is so much more than a utilitarian object. In Randi's home even the simple chore of making butter was invested with a special effort to create something beautiful. That was her legacy to all of us. Life was hard, and there was no end of work for farm women in her time, yet all of her girls were taught to prepare food that was appealing as well as nourishing and serve it on well-appointed tables. Clothing, though mostly hand-made was beautifully sewn and linens were trimmed with hand-made lace.

I hope that fifty years from now someone in our family will be looking at the butter mold as they read this story and appreciate what it represents as much as I do.

❧

Part Six:

The Ingredients

My Parents

My father, William Lee Ferdon

*M*y father was the fourth child and the first boy born to the Ferdons. He was born in Worthington, Minnesota on November 23, 1902. Grandma was thrilled with her first son and doted on him. Grandpa was glad to finally have a boy to help with the haying, as well as carry on the family name. The girls in the family were educated to become teachers, but the boys were put to work for Grandpa after they finished eighth grade. My father had no opportunity to attend school beyond that. At one time, he told me he had wanted to become a veterinarian, but Grandpa wasn't willing to let him go on with his education.

Dad was quick thinking, quick moving, quick tempered, and hardworking. He was given to tirades and tantrums over seemingly trivial matters, such as arriving home to a room cluttered with children's playthings. Perhaps this stemmed from frustration at never finding his niche in life. Restless and easily bored, he rarely stuck with any job for long, and usually managed to avoid taking responsibility for his actions, choosing to move on rather than face the consequences of his mistakes. Certainly he was fiscally irresponsible, but conversely was generous and unfailingly willing to help someone in need.

During the depression years, after his father died and his business had died with him, Dad worked long hours for little money at whatever work was available. He was resourceful, and for a time he bought horses that could be described as "nags," improved their appearance with grooming and feeding and took them to outlying areas to sell. He took a circuitous route on the return trip to avoid encounters with customers who realized they had made a bad purchase.

He established himself early in life as an aggressive salesman, but he was an easy target for any salesman who appeared at our door. He loved to read, and any book salesmen was sure to make a sale to Dad. I was happy for every volume of the quality choices he purchased. I particularly made excellent use of the reference books, huge dictionary, and world atlas. The dictionary was expensive at twenty five dollars, a great amount for us to spend on a book. Mother made such a fuss about the price, we referred to it laughingly as "The Twenty Five Dollar Job" for the rest of our childhood. I believe the dictionary still graces a shelf in Wanda's library.

Dad took time to play with me and let me tag along to the garden or to work on the car. He seemed to enjoy having me around. He took us fishing, picnicking, and on Sunday drives to some of the many lakes in the area to play in the water. Dad's encouragement and approval were blessings to me. I felt I could not do anything to please my mother. She seemed to feel if she gave us a pat on the back by way of encouragement, we would become overbearing and conceited.

When the grandchildren came along, Dad enjoyed them as much, or more, than his own children. He had more time to spend with them and gave them his undivided attention. He particularly loved to build toys for them from wood or sheet metal.

Mother and Dad moved from Duluth to Minneapolis when Dad was sent to a rehab center there following hip replacement surgery in 1958. The surgical procedure was relatively new, and had not been entirely successful. He was expected to be confined to a wheelchair, but through great determination, he was soon walking with crutches and finally with a cane. Eventually, he rarely used the cane. He went back to work as a salesman in an appliance store in Minneapolis where he and Mother lived until she died in 1981. After retirement, Dad worked as a volunteer at a senior center. In 1987 we moved him back to Duluth where he died at Park Point Manor Nursing Home on July 3, 1987.

                                        ∽

My Mother, Alice Odella (Heieie) Ferdon

Mother was the third youngest child of the Heieies. She was strong in spirit, proud, and a little vain. She spoke Norwegian before she learned English. Much of her excellent schooling in grammar, spelling, and writing was provided by her sister, Alma who taught in the country school Mother attended. Unfortunately, Mother taught us no Norwegian, except for a few songs. Many immigrants to America at that time were proud to become citizens and speak the language spoken by Americans, and so they had no desire to teach their children the language they had left behind. Another reason I believed she did not care to have us learn Norwegian was that she and her sisters lapsed into the tongue of their childhood when they wanted to discuss matters they preferred the children didn't hear.

Mother was a great story teller, and we begged her to tell stories with "trimmings," which meant she embellished the old familiar fairy tales with her own twists that would have us roaring with laughter. In Mother's version of *Cinderella*, all sorts of accidents befell the wicked stepsisters, and the witch in *Snow White* got her comeuppance. We loved to hear her tell stories in Norwegian, and she did make an exception to retell the stories of her childhood as her mother had told them to her. Our favorite was *Billy Goats Gruff*, which our own children clamored to hear a generation later. When Mother came to visit, my children liked to invite their friends in to listen to her tell this story. They loved it as much as we had.

Like her sister, Olette, Mother loved needlework, and we still have some of her creations. Fortunately, I had passed some of these treasures on to our children and so they escaped the fire that destroyed our home in 2003.

Mother was an excellent seamstress and could make clothing from tissue paper patterns of her own creation. If she needed some nice fabric to make one of us a special dress, she simply went to her trunk and selected one of her dresses saved from earlier, carefree times, took it apart and created an original design. When I was about five years old, I wanted so much to sew things on her old White treadle machine. In spite of the many demands on her time, she patiently sat me on her lap and taught me to operate the machine, guiding my inept fingers while she treadled.

We rarely ate anyplace but at home so we took Mother's great cooking for granted. It was wonderful to come home from school and smell homemade soup bubbling on the old iron cookstove with bread baking in the oven.

Every few days she baked four loaves of bread and often an added treat of cinnamon rolls. Meals were served nicely in the dining room on pretty tablecloths even when linens had to be washed by hand in water hauled from the well and heated on the stove.

In the matter of religious training, Alice was a stickler. Our uncle Nils Njus and his brother influenced the family's rigid religious upbringing which set the stage for our training. We were sent to the strictest Lutheran church-es Mother could find, within the walls of which little joy or solace existed. For many years, I resented her subjecting us to this harsh teaching based in fear. I finally came to understand it was simply because it was so ingrained in her from childhood. There came a time after I had grown up when she took comfort in attending my kinder, gentler Lutheran Church with me.

Mother remained bright and active through most of her life, despite a time when she took to her bed for a year or so in mid-life. Her good spirits returned and stayed with her until she suffered a heart attack and died in Minneapolis at the age of eighty one.

∾

The author's sister Wanda and brother Jerry.

The author between brother Jerry and sister Wanda.

Sisters Wanda, Vonnie, and Donna Ferdon

My Father's Family,
the Ferdons

My Paternal Grandfather,
George Timothy Ferdon

*M*y paternal grandfather, George Ferdon was born in Wild Rose, Wisconsin on March 18, 1871. He married my Grandmother, Caroline Congdon on March 5, 1889. Grandpa died on August 29, 1932, one year before I was born. The following memories of him have been related to me by my parents, my grandmother, and my brother, Jerry, who is my only sibling who remembers him. According to my mother, he was handsome and hard working, and flared into tirades of temper at the least provocation. He operated a livery stable in Glenwood, Minnesota, and owned a hay bailing operation.

Since his first three children were daughters, undoubtedly Grandpa was happy when my father was born in 1902. He finally had a son to help in the hay business, as well as carry on the family name. The daughters had sons, but they did not bear his name.

Grandpa bid on the hay crops of local farmers and then baled the hay crops he purchased, which he resold. Jerry remembers Mother and Dad working at the various farms during haying season. Mother cooked for Grandpa's crews employed to do the cutting and bailing.

Grandpa had expected his sons to spend their lives farming and baling hay as he had. Therefore, they were taken out of school to work for him after completing eighth grade. Unfortunately, after Grandpa's death the business was gone and his sons were left to find whatever work they could in the midst of a depression.

When Grandpa was dying of stomach cancer, he asked to see Jerry, the apple of his eye. Jerry was about six at the time, and he did not recognize the thin and ravaged invalid that had been his Grandpa. He began to cry and ran from the room in fear. As he related this event to me he still felt guilty thinking he had hurt his grandpa's feelings.

∽

My Paternal Grandmother,
Caroline Esther Olive Congdon Ferdon

My Grandma Ferdon was the only grandparent I knew. Mother's parents died when I was very young, and my Grandfather Ferdon was gone before I was born. Grandma was born in 1866 to Benjamin Congdon and Olive Frisby Congdon in Binghamton, New York. At the age of five, she moved with her family to Worthington, Minnesota, on the first passenger train that came into the area.

I was fortunate to obtain from a cousin a copy of the beginning of a book of poetry written at age fourteen by Grandma's Aunt Caroline for whom she was named. When I received this poetry in the mail, it was interesting to recall Grandma expressing a keen interest in simple poems I wrote as a child. I had written these verses in pencil in a small notebook purchased with a precious nickel on a Saturday evening trip to Long Prairie.

She never told me about her aunt who wrote poetry, but she finally asked me if she could have the poems I had written. I was pleased that she liked them and gladly gave her the small collection. Perhaps she fancied her grandchild had the potential to become a poet like her Aunt Carrie. Carrie died at age fourteen shortly after her book of poetry was published.

Grandma Ferdon was the only person ever to care for us outside of our parents. She came to stay with us for a visit each summer and on the rare occasions when Mother and Dad had to be away. At the time of my birth,

Grandma was at our home to help Mother, and actually ushered me into the world when the doctor failed to arrive in time. There wasn't much Grandma couldn't cope with.

Strict and hard-bitten (to which her photo will attest) we loved her because she was Grandma. She had five children and spent part of the year with each of them after Grandpa's death. During her visits, she taught my sisters and me to do needlework, which I appreciated and I continue to enjoy the benefits of those lessons.

As Mother and Grandma worked around the house during her visits, Mother was treated to a rundown on the transgressions of other family members, to which Mom would make noncommittal responses. We all knew our failings would be reported to the next family she visited. Mother would simply tell us, "Just let it go in one ear and out the other."

We hoped the other families did the same.

Grandma lived in Benson, Minnesota, as did most of Dad's family. After we moved from Long Prairie to Duluth, it was necessary for Grandma to take the train to visit us. When she was due to arrive, we all trouped to the train depot to greet her with dutiful kisses. Rotund in figure, barely over five feet tall, she somehow cut an imposing figure as she disembarked with her serviceable black leather handbag over her arm, carrying the shoe-box tied with string that had contained her lunch. She wore or carried (depending on the weather) a long black coat under which she was dressed in one of a collection of home-sewn, floral print dresses. Her dresses appeared to have been created from the same pattern as they were uniform in style, except the dressier ones boasted lace collars. Her footwear was chosen for comfort rather than style; sensible black lace-up shoes with medium heels.

Grandma had not, to my knowledge, ever cut her hair. It reached below her waist when she took out the tortoise-shell hairpins to release it from a rather unattractive bun on top of her head to begin her nightly ritual of brushing and braiding the salt-and-pepper tresses. Shampooing was a tedious procedure, and I wondered why she invested such pride and maintenance in a less than appealing feature.

Her jewelry was a string of graduated jet beads and her wedding ring, a wide gold band set in a curious design of tiny turquoise stones.

On the rare occasions I visited Grandma in her small upstairs apartment in Benson, she served simple meals on Blue Willow china. I liked being at Grandma's for supper and later chose Blue Willow for my kitchen china. When a cousin came to visit me a few years ago and saw the table set with Blue Willow, she remembered too.

"It's just like going to Grandma's for supper,'" she declared.

Grandma's summer visits continued into my high school years before she became too infirm to travel.

She was fond of saying to us when we were young, "You'd better hug me while you can. You never know how long I'll be around."

In spite of her concern that her days were numbered, Grandma lived to be ninety four before she died in a Wheaton, Minnesota nursing home.

∽

Lillian Caroline (Ferdon) Knutson

Lillie was the first child born to Caroline and George Ferdon. She was born on May 21, 1890 at Bigelow, Minnesota. As she grew up, she bore a striking likeness to her mother, and appeared to share Grandma's strong personality and stern disposition. I cannot remember a time when I saw Aunt Lillie smile.

She married Amos Knutson and had a family of six children. The first child, Ella died at eighteen months and the second, Lois, died at six months. Their other four children were Vernon, Iona, Lowell, and LaVonne. I did not know this family well, but Jerry recalls visiting them in Benson as a child. Amos was resourceful and a good provider, who adjusted to the depression by using his newly purchased truck to develop a delivery service for the citizens of Benson. Jerry liked visiting the Knutsons because the children had some fine toys. He especially remembered their toy trucks.

Iona and her husband, Delmar, visited us in Duluth several times. Their daughter, Sharon, still keeps in touch and visits me when she can.

∽

Olive Lorinda (Ferdon) Burbank

The second child of Caroline and George Ferdon was my Aunt Olive, born on December 1, 1897 at Worthington, Minnesota. Educated to be a teacher,

Aunt Olive was intelligent, creative, and capable. She was quick to anger when provoked, and received plenty of provocation from her husband, Lawrence Burbank. Uncle Larry was an ex-boxer who, despite his charm and generosity, tried the patience of his family. A problem drinker from an early age, he made life difficult for his wife and children.

The children were close in age to my siblings and me. The family lived in Benson, a reasonable distance to travel for visits, so we came to know them better than the other cousins. Jimmy was the oldest, followed by Betty, Jackie, Joanne, and Janie. When they grew up and married, the girls moved far from Benson. Jackie, after being discharged from the Navy, became a heavy drinker and finally was not heard from by any of the family. We do not know his whereabouts. Jimmy stayed in Benson for a number of years, coming to visit us regularly in Duluth. Upon retirement, he moved to Colorado. He returned to Minnesota in 2005.

My husband particularly liked pheasant hunting in Benson with my brother and dad. On those occasions, he enjoyed staying with Aunt Olive and Uncle Larry, who treated him as one of their own. By then, Uncle Larry had joined A.A. and was good company. Aunt Olive died in Benson in 1989 a few years after Larry's death.

⌒

Jeanette Rose (Ferdon) Donaldson

Born in Worthington, Minnesota on October 31, 1899, Aunt Jeanette (Peggy) was the same age as my mother. I did not really know her (except through descriptions by Mother and Grandma) until I was an adult and visited her in Minneapolis where she had lived since her marriage to Clarence Donaldson. They had three children, Gladys, Forrest, and Marilyn. Aunt Peggy was the only mother in our family to pursue a full time career. She was a teacher, but later worked at the Honeywell Corporation in a supervisory position. Her granddaughter Sandy (Forrest's child) is currently compiling a genealogy of the Ferdon family.

By the time I had my children, Uncle Clarence had acquired a hunting lodge on the Gunflint Trail off the North Shore of Lake Superior, which brought him to Duluth often and gave us an opportunity to become better acquainted with him and Aunt Peggy. They were favorites of my entire family.

Uncle Clarence was the first person we knew to undergo lung surgery as a result of smoking. Although he survived the surgery, his breathing was seriously impaired. When Uncle Clarence died some years later, Aunt Peggy moved to Huntingon Beach, California where her daughter Marilyn lived. She died in a nursing home there in 1993.

‿

Glen Eugene Ferdon

Glen was the youngest child of Caroline and George, who were happy to have another son. Born March 10, 1904, Glen was an adorable child and Grandma doted on him. Glen married a pretty woman named Gertie Simonsen who presented him with two daughters, Connie and Gwendolyn. On her summer visits with us, Grandma often spoke of the family's problems, blaming Gertie for Glen's failings as a husband and father.

We occasionally visited with them in Benson when I was young, but Mother disapproved of Uncle Glen's drinking. Self-indulgence led to his alcohol addiction and early demise. Unfortunately, Gertie had preceded him to the grave leaving the two girls with a father who couldn't care for them.

Uncle Glen visited us once in Duluth when he was in his early forties after he was widowed and his children placed in foster homes. He was still a handsome man, sober now, and seemed very much the gentleman. He died in Benson on August 12, 1949 shortly after that visit.

I don't know where Connie is, but Mother and Dad heard from Gwen while they lived in Minneapolis. Gwen died of cancer shortly thereafter.

On a lighter note, the Ferdon family photo shows a sweet-faced Glen seated on grandpa's lap, after having just pulled his brother's hair and messing it up just as the picture was taken. The photo proved to be the best of all family members (except for Dad's hair) so the photographer printed several copies of another shot, cut out Dad's head and glued it over the bad hair in the selected pose.

We have begged my brother, who has the original photo, for a peek under the pasted-on head, but he steadfastly refuses to try removing the head for fear of ruining the photo.

∾

Olive (Ferdon) Burbank and her
husband, Lawrence.

Jeanette (Ferdon) Donaldson with her
husband, Clarence, and their
first child, Gladys.

The George and Caroline (Congdon) Ferdon family; (left to right),
Jeanette, Caroline, Olive, Lillian, George (holding Glen), and William.

My Mother's family, the Heieies

My Maternal Grandfather, Gunnilius Heieie

My mother's father, Gunnilius Heieie, was one of three brothers born in Northwestern Minnesota to Norwegian immigrants. The name is pronounced Hi-Yí. I have heard a few versions of the origin of the name, but the one found by a cousin who is working on a genealogy chart for the family seems the most authentic. When small haystacks (or hummocks) of hay are collected from the fields, small spots remain in the field where each stack had been piled. These places in the field were called heieies.

In 1905, Grandpa acquired one hundred and sixty acres of homestead land near Greenbush, Minnesota, a small town near Roseau. According to my mother, Grandpa suffered terrible headaches and generally had a hard time coping with life, the demands of the farm, and a family of nine children. He dealt harshly with his children and I expect was disappointed that the first eight were girls. Farmers depended on having sons to help with the chores. His ninth child was the only son born to the Heieies.

The harshness of farming and raising children took a terrible toll on the settlers in this unfriendly climate; it is hard to imagine my grandparents ever being young and fun-loving. Yet, I had in my possession at one time elaborate greeting cards from 1884 sent by Grandpa to Randi in their courting days. They were very romantic and full of hearts and flowers, declaring his love without, I am sure, any thought of the hardships in store.

When the children were grown, Grandma and Grandpa moved to a home in Monticello, Minnesota, where they lived to celebrate their Golden Wedding Anniversary in 1934, the year after I was born.

⤶

My Maternal Grandmother, Randi Odden Heieie

My maternal grandmother, Randi Odden, came to America from Trondheim, Norway in 1867 with her parents, Andre and Kari, and two sisters, Martha and Caroline. Mother recalled being told of the ocean crossing. The ship encountered such severe weather that the three year old Randi became dangerously seasick and was close to dying. Her family had among their possessions a small trunk which they decided to use for an ocean burial. Obviously, that did not become necessary, but I always think of this story when someone comments on the hardships endured by immigrants who came to America during that period.

Randi's character is revealed in descriptions of her husband and children as her family is the story of her life. I did not have an opportunity to know her but believe she must have been a special person as her son-in-law (my father) often declared her to be a saint. I do not believe Dad was held in great favor by this traditional Norwegian family, especially Gunnilius. Perhaps Randi looked on Dad a little more kindly.

Randi's wedding picture shows her in a dress of deep red shot-silk over white silk and lace with a lace headpiece. Before my home burned, I had the overdress which had been saved by my aunt. This was all that remained of the wedding finery as Randi had used the white fabric and the lace to make over into clothing for her children.

I often wished I had known this grandmother, and wondered how well my mother really knew her.

⤶

Claudina (Heieie) Njus

Claudina was the first child born to the Heieies. I was unable to learn much about her as she had left home by the time Mother was born. I have no pictures of Claudina. We know she married Nils Njus, a preacher, and gave birth to five sons. I met only her eldest child, Julian, who came with his wife to visit us in Duluth when I was young. They lived in Chicago at that time.

I did not ask Julian about his family because I knew he had been troubled through his life by a tragic event which occurred in his childhood. Claudina had left him with his baby brother in a high chair while she went to tend to chores in the barn. A fire started in the house, and although Julian was rescued, his brother could not be saved.

Claudina had three more boys, but never recovered from her loss in the fire. She became ill with breast cancer and died before she could raise her children.

I was interested in the fate of the remaining children, but discussion of the Njus tragedy was avoided by the family.

⤙

Olette Heieie

Olette was the second child in the Heieie family, and remained unmarried after losing her fiance in the first World War. I had an opportunity to know Aunt Olette, as I saw her at least once a year during my childhood. She was a shy, a quiet, gentle, caring lady. I expect she helped Grandma with the housekeeping and care of some of the younger children, as she remained at home with her parents for a number of years before moving into a home with Aunt Alma who also remained single.

Olette worked at Anchor Hospital in St. Paul during most of her adult life and cared for the home she shared with Alma, while Alma devoted her time to helping their parents and other family members. Olette loved needlework and created beautiful embroidered and crocheted linens.

In all the time I knew her, I do not remember a time when she complained or said an unkind word about anyone. We looked forward to the visits from Alma and Olette. We knew they would come bearing gifts, not the least of which were their unfailing love and acceptance.

⤆

Ella (Heieie) Olson Warnes

I saw Aunt Ella only in photos until I was in high school when she came to Duluth for a visit. I knew she had lost her first husband years before I was born. According to Mother, he had been struck by lightning as he drove in his horse and buggy.

Aunt Ella was remarried, and the Warnes family moved to Bremerton, Washington, around 1940. She had a family of seven, only one of whom I had met until this year (2006) when I found Ella's youngest child, Vivian Sutton, who lives in Georgia. She is close to my age and we enjoy corresponding by letter and telephone. I am grateful for this opportunity to become acquainted with her and also hope to learn more about Aunt Ella and other family members through our visits.

⤆

Alma Pauline Heieie

Along with Aunt Olette, Alma was best known to us of all Mother's family. She was a positive influence in all of our lives. She was determined to educate herself and others in her family and improve the lives of all of them. She worked her way through high school and teachers college and taught school for a few years before attending business college in Superior, Wisconsin to learn stenography. She worked for room and board wherever she attended school in addition to maintaining her class and study schedule. During her years of teaching, she had some of her younger siblings in her classes, and made certain they developed excellent basic skills in reading, writing, spelling, and math.

She was to discover that her cooking and baking skills would provide her with a far better income than anything she else she had studied. She combined her organizational skills with her ability as a chef and turned her efforts to housekeeping in large homes. Through her hard work she was able to provide a home for herself and Olette, a home for their parents, and an education for her brother at the University of Minnesota.

Though Alma died in 1975 at the age of eighty one, we continue to see living proof of this amazing woman's influence in the newest generation of our family.

⤳

Hannah Heieie (married name unknown)

I have no photos of Hannah, the fifth daughter of the family. She died at an early age under tragic circumstances. Because of the age span, Mother did not know Hannah very well, but told me of her unhappy marriage to a man whose name I do not know. The short-lived union ended abruptly when Hannah was found dead with a razor in her hand, an apparent suicide. The loss of this daughter was overwhelming to Grandma, the circumstances of her death an added burden to the pain of losing a child.

Mother remembered watching from the window as her mother left the house to work in the barn and seeing her fall to the ground to give way to the grief she did not want her children to witness. In that houseful of children, Grandma could not even find a place to weep in private.

Some years later, the mother or sister of Hannah's husband, in a deathbed confession, admitted that she was involved in Hannah's death. Though horrifying, I thought if this knowledge had come earlier, my Grandmother might at least have been spared the specter of suicide which added such pain to her grief.

⤳

Gina (Heieie) Giddings

Gina did not seem to take life as seriously as the other sisters. This sixth child appeared to me as breezy and fun-loving. She married Art Giddings and moved to an island home on Lake of the Woods, where Uncle Art owned and operated a ferry, "The Scout," on which he carried passengers from islands to the mainland. The Giddings had two sons, Gail and Wally, who were bright and good company. We became better acquainted with the boys in our adult lives. In later years, after Uncle Art had died, both Aunt Gina and Gail lived in Minneapolis, where we often visited our parents. This gave us an opportunity to see the Giddings more than we had in earlier years.

As was the case with most of the Heieie family, Gina died of heart disease in her early eighties, a few years after Alma died.

↬

Olga (Heieie) Vanderford

Olga was the youngest girl in the Heieie family. She was beautiful and could have been Mother's twin, except she was not as trim-figured as Alice. The physical resemblance was where the similarity between the two sisters ended, and Mother did not like to hear anyone exclaim over the remarkable physical likeness.

I was not exactly sure why, but the sisters reverted to Norwegian when Olga's name came up in conversation. This was a sure indication, coupled with their raised brows and eye-rolling, that the news was not good. Things never seemed to be going well with Olga, at least in their opinion.

Olga did not look directly at anyone when she spoke to them, which even as a child made me uneasy. Her hair was unsuitably long, frizzy and a little unkempt looking, while the lovely face was garishly made up with badly applied cosmetics. I recall when we were kids how we squirmed as she swooped down on us with her greeting embrace with its overwhelming odor of perfume applied too heavily.

After divorcing her first husband (divorce was of course frowned upon by the family) she married Bob Vanderford. Bob had been a prisoner in the second World War, and had a gaunt haunted appearance. They lived in Chisago City, Minnesota, and showed up to visit in Duluth with some regularity as Bob also had relatives here. Neither of the Vanderfords ever seemed to work at anything, and I have no idea how they subsisted.

Olga died in a Minneapolis hospital some years before her older sisters.

↬

Marion T. Heieie

Marion was the youngest child and the only son in Mother's family. Doted on by the entire family, it is surprising he was not dreadfully spoiled. He was blonde, blue-eyed, tall, and handsome. Bright and gifted at drawing and painting, he seemed a natural to study art, had that been considered an appropriate option by the family. He contented himself with pursuing it as a hobby and chose to study dentistry at the University of Minnesota.

Uncle Marion visited us with Alma and Olette through the years. I found him to be patient and kind with an even temperament and droll sense of humor. He showed no sign of being the pampered youngest child and only son among eight daughters.

He practiced dentistry for many years in Minneapolis where he lived with his wife, LaFaye, in Minnetonka until his retirement. At that time, he and LaFaye returned to her hometown of Brookings, South Dakota. He taught at the university in Brookings for some time after his retirement, and maintained a youthful appearance and outlook, tending his gardens and painting in watercolor. His favorite still life subjects were the flowers he grew. When I saw him last he was in his eighties and still appeared much younger than his years. He was the longest living member of the family; well past ninety when he died in 2004. LaFaye had been ill for many years, and died within a year of Marion.

The author's paternal grandfather, Gunnilius Heieie (right), with his brothers.

The author's maternal Grandmother, Randi (standing at right), with her family (left to right) sisters Martha and Caroline, father Andre, and mother Kari Odden.

The author's maternal aunt Ella (Heieie) Warnes with her husband Anton and their children.

The author's aunt Gina Giddings (left)
with her sisters Olga Vanderford, Olette Heieie, and Alma Heieie.

The author's uncle, Marion Heieie,
with his wife, LaFaye.

The author's aunt Alma Heieie.

My Family

Author Donna Schilling and her husband, Hartley, at their wedding.

Hartley and Donna Schilling in 1988.

*Donna and Hartley Schilling
at their fiftieth eedding anniversary..*

The author's son, Hartley Schilling, at 26 in 1979.

The author's daughter, Dawn Schilling, at 16 in 1972.